A Head for Running

William Sichel

A Head for Running

Inside my ultra-marathon triumphs and disasters

by William Sichel

Published by The Orcadian (Kirkwall Press) 2022
Hell's Half Acre, Hatston, Kirkwall, Orkney, KW15 1GJ
Tel. 01856 879000 • Fax 01856 879001 • www.orcadian.co.uk

Book sales: www.orcadian.co.uk/shop/index.php

ISBN 978-1-912889-27-3

Printed in Orkney by The Orcadian, Hatston Print Centre, Hell's Half Acre, Hatston, Kirkwall, Orkney, KW15 1GJ

Contents

Dedication

I want to dedicate this book to my late wife, Elizabeth, without whose consistent love, support and approval I wouldn't have gone far during our 35 years together. We got together on a whim, in very unusual circumstances and for some unknown reason it worked for both of us.

Elizabeth had no interest in sport unless I was doing it. Having told her, on meeting in 1982, that my sporting life was over, she had to cope with a totally unexpected resurgence of my sporting dreams and a new passion in my life. This she did with great stoicism and unwavering support and I will be forever grateful to her, for that.

She is very much missed.

Acknowledgements

To my daughters Tanya and Bella, for your love and understanding when growing up with a Dad who did crazy running events.

To Jessica Jones for her cheerful love, support and encouragement during the arduous writing process and for inspiring the book's title.

To the members of 'Team Sichel' who kept me on the road for so many years. In no particular order: David Murrie, who has provided coaching and sports science advice. Rebecca Dent, high performance dietitian. Alan Young, Tim Rainey, Adrian Stott, Marja Hardus, Bella Sichel, Peter Witting, Wendy Edwards and Erica Clarkson who provided crew support. Without you the performances couldn't have happened. Dr Les Hall, my chiropractor. Masseurs Dave Walker and more recently Teenie Cromarty; and to Shaun Brassfield-Thorpe (strength and conditioning).

My friends and statisticians Andy Milroy, Adrian Stott and Alan Young, who helped with the arduous task of collating and organising my records.

To my sponsors, especially the local ones, without whose help and support I wouldn't have been able to get to many of my far-off races.

To the many race organisers, who provided these extreme events for me to test myself.

To Alf Shacklady for demonstrating what can still be achieved well into your 80's.

To my editor, James Miller, for your willingness to take on this project, your polite patience with a complete novice and your kind encouragement through the many months of writing this book.

And finally to the people of Orkney and the Sanday community in particular, for their quiet support and interest in my seemingly insane exploits.

Ultra running is often a case of 'mind over matter' and gutting it out! (Picture: Alan Young).

Foreword

I stand accused in chapter one of setting William on a slippery slope beyond the marathon into the world of Ultra Running. I am guilty as charged!

As William explains, this arose from phone conversations we developed pre internet days when he used to call the running shop I managed in Edinburgh from `Orkney, to ask about and order running shoes!

In those intervening years, in which William has become a very good friend, he has never ceased to amaze me how he always embraces new challenges both in his personal life and his running life.

His approach was never "Why should I do this?" Always the "Why shouldn't I do this?"

"What do I have to do to achieve this goal?" Doing the research to find out who has the expertise he could reach out to…then looking at his own strengths and weakness and asking "How am I going to do this?"

William is also a classic example of not giving in to age. To him age is not a barrier, age is just a number. As he has got older, and inevitably a little slower, he has just embraced different challenges, which generally involved going long and culminating in the fascinating race that is the Sri Chinmoy 3,100 mile race, where he became the oldest finisher of that special event a few months after his 60th birthday.

We live in a time when so many people, maybe related to the pandemic experience, are seeking out new challenges and new boundaries. It is true that these challenges are all relative and one runner's first Park Run is another runner's first championship medal or GB vest.

William's journey is running marathons and then running them better. Moving to ultras, not just for the pure physical joy of running, which is a big part of it, more just the overwhelming love of setting boundaries and breaking them. Add to that, the sheer consistency over many years of running at such a high level in whatever event he was aiming for….for Scotland and then GB at 100 km and 24 hours with distinction ..winning team medals internationally and British championships and setting a whole host of records along the way.

William is a shining example of someone who has been setting his own boundaries for the last 20-30 years and surpassing these boundaries regularly, in many cases. Not with a desire to say "look at me I am wonderful" as many do these days, but because it is the whole raison d'aitre for living.

Within these chapters, as well as chronicling many inspiring running achievements, William weaves his own very personal life stories too. Moving to the islands and the struggle to start a completely new life and talking of love and loss, all inter-weaved and continually showing the inner resilience that turns "perceived problems into new realities.'

Williams' story is as much an inner journey as an outer journey. The outer journey is chronicled in times, distances and dates on this day or that year, but the inner journey is also running parallel, living in the moment, from moment to moment looking for and finding an ever deeper meaning and fulfillment to life.

Whatever your sport, or if you have never done any serious exercise in your life, William's story is one of perseverance to achieve goals, while also being able to enjoy the journey along the way. It is sure to inspire you to try and raise the bar a little in your own life.

Adrian Tarit Stott

Edinburgh

August 2022

Getting started

... 'I'll give it a go' ...

My first training run, if you can call it that, in my modern sporting era, was on April 12, 1992. The date is easy to remember, because I saw the London Marathon at home on TV, then went and jogged 'round the block'. I lived in the far north of Scotland on a fairly remote island called Sanday, in Orkney, so 'round the block' actually meant down a single track road for a mile or so, then up a grassy track and finally on to a gravel farm road and back to my house, a small croft called Upper Breckan.

I say 'my modern sporting era' as I had, in a previous life, been heavily involved in sport, albeit it was table tennis. But watching the London Marathon that day on TV was the trigger that got me out the door and led to a 26 year career in long distance running which saw me complete 110 ultra-marathons (winning 18 of them) in 22 countries and represent both Scotland and Great Britain on 12 occasions. I went on to cover over 25,000 miles in races alone, becoming a national champion and multiple world record holder.

When I jogged 'round the block' that day in 1992 I had no ambitions as a runner at that time. I didn't suddenly get the urge to 'do the London Marathon'. Up to that point I had run for about two weeks every year in the lead up to representing the Sanday team in the North Isles Sports Day – a keenly contested annual competition between several of the small, outer North Isles of the Orkney archipelago. The host island rotated each year and the running events were usually held on a 300m grass track. I always appeared in the 1500m as nobody else wanted to do it and I won it once.

Aged 38, I wasn't overweight or unfit. Far from it. I'd done ten years hard labour, re-building Upper Breckan, starting various businesses and trying to get established in Sanday. Fortunately, I had a very hard-working wife, Elizabeth, by my side to share the burden.

My original aim for running was purely relief, getting away from the stress and strain of attempting to develop a sustainable way of life on a far-off northern isle in Orkney. Countless ideas had floundered due to the paucity of communication with the outside world. Back then, in the early 1980s and long before Internet and email, the 'lifeline' ferry called into Sanday just three times every week. The post took forever. I simply needed a break from it all, even if it was just 20 minutes, a few times a week.

I started running regularly, increasing the distances, and really enjoyed it.

It's hard to convey the sense of isolation I felt in those days, with virtually no access to any information about running or training or contact with other runners for that matter.

My first official race in Orkney was the Hoy Half-marathon two months later, in June, 1992. The post-race buzz gave me the thrill of competition that I didn't realise I had been missing, for the previous ten years. Looking back over my subsequent 110 ultra-marathons, ten marathons and three half-marathons, it might appear that I had some overall plan. This couldn't be further from the truth.

When running became my passion, it was important to me, that it impinged as little as possible on my family life. This just satisfied a gut feeling I had and wasn't imposed by Elizabeth. She wasn't a morning person at all and struggled to get up by 8am on six days a week, and had a long lie on Sunday until 10am. I was very much an early bird, so for many years I was able to be 'all done' training-wise by the time Elizabeth emerged into the day.

Finishing my first London Marathon on Westminster Bridge in April, 1993

Initially, I had no special gym or facility available to me, so I just used my animal shed. Not ideal, but it got me going in those early years. Five years later, in 1997, we had a large, timber-framed, sectional building erected on a concrete base. One part was reserved as my new gym and accommodated training equipment as my running ambitions advanced. It was also converted into a "climate chamber" to mimic forthcoming race venues such as Death Valley in California.

Once I'd done a couple of half-marathons, I realised I had 'something' that enabled me to run well and I enjoyed it hugely. I then set my sights on being able to compete at the marathon again - I had run one marathon in 1981, a year prior to moving to Orkney – and between 1992 and 1996 I went on to run eight of them, my best being London in 1995.

Money was always very tight in those days and I was adamant that my involvement in running would not put pressure on the meagre family budget. Elizabeth actually made me a complete set of foul-weather running gear, on her sewing machine. We had bought the material by mail order and off she went.

As my ambitions grew, the shortage of cash was a huge stimulus to try and find some form of sponsorship from local companies which might be interested in supporting my burgeoning running journey. Although the idea of putting my head above the parapet and asking for money was anathema to me, it simply had to be done. I was incredibly lucky when my own accountants, Price & Long, agreed to cover my running expenses for 12 months. This was a huge boost and enabled me to travel to a range of events, without it impinging on the family housekeeping.

Living so remotely, it was clear to me, from very early on, that I had to plan and prepare for travelling to races very carefully. My journeys would often start with a ferry journey from Sanday to Kirkwall then, usually, an overnight stay, up early the next day and then a bus to another ferry across to mainland Scotland and then buses and trains to my destination. In terms of time, Sanday to Edinburgh, say, is 24 hours.

When I competed down south, I had access to bookshops and, more importantly, other runners and started to get some insight into what competitors were doing. I also discovered *Athletics Weekly* magazine and became a subscriber.

In those days, the vogue was to log huge training mileages to be successful at the marathon and ultra-endurance events. I can clearly remember an *Athletics Weekly* front page story, about a runner called John Downes, who was running over 150 miles a week in training. Many of the athletes I met before races were clocking up around a 100 miles a week and more. The odd thing was, I was beating them!

Did I get sucked into the high-mileage mania?

Yes, I did.

For a couple of years I tried to reach a 100 miles a week training schedule but never managed it. I was severely limited, not only by the time I had available to train, but also by the lack of daylight in the winter months. Located on the 59th parallel latitude, Sanday shares a northerly position, similar to that of Oslo in Norway and St Petersburg in Russia. I had no headlamp of any description and I couldn't take time off during the day, so I peaked at around the 70 – 80 miles at best.

I enjoyed the marathon distance, but noticed that I wasn't exhausted at the finish. This comment was picked up by an experienced ultra-runner, Adrian Stott, who suggested I try an ultra. I subsequently won my first 100km race (a little more than two marathons in distance) in the 1994 Scottish Championships.

After a couple of years, I made the decision to tilt my training more toward intensity, than volume. This was a major decision and one I have stuck with all my sporting life. I did this, at the time, by starting to run with a weight vest. The reasoning seemed sound to me and the evidence I got back from myself, in the way of performances, was also very sound.

I maintained the same running speed, despite the extra load; this then made that same speed 'feel easier' when competing without the vest. I should point out that I was considered a 'crank' at the time for training in this way and quickly learned not to mention my training methods and my low mileage to anybody. I knew these techniques worked for me and that was all that mattered.

The design of my weight vests varied a lot over the 20 years I used them. Often the design was changed in order to make them more comfortable, and yes, Elizabeth's sewing machine came in handy, yet again. The most common extra load I wore, was about 5 per cent of my body weight. In later years, I experimented with loads up to 10 per cent, to see if that made any performance difference. I only stopped using my trusty weight vest because I developed a slight right hip injury, which only manifested itself when I wore it.

However, by then, I had been incredibly toughened, mentally and physically to the rigours of running long distances. I went from strength to strength and made my debut for the Great Britain 100km Team in Moscow, in May, 1996. From then on, I was a regular in the GB team until 2000.

It was fellow teammate, Don Ritchie, one of the all-time great 100km and 100 mile runners, who suggested I try other ultra-distance events, such as the 24-hour event.

"Slot them in at the end of the season" he suggested. I took his advice and ran my first 24-hour track race in September, 1996, winning it at my first attempt. This victory gave me a huge boost and encouraged me to focus on 24-hour races on road and track from 2000 onward.

My best ever 24-hour run came in Basel, Switzerland, in 2000. When I stood at the start line, I had six years of high level, 100km running in my legs from 18 races, which had honed my pace over these long distances. I won the Basel race with 153 miles / 246 kms.

I was now thinking about tackling longer and longer distances … unimaginable distances.

My attitude always was "I'll give it a go" …

Disaster in Eastern Europe

... 'she alerted the race doctor' ...

It was 2004, I was leading the race. I was excited. It was my first 48 hour indoor event. I was in the far east of the Czech Republic in the Moravian capital, Brno. The race venue was a huge exhibition centre. The track consisted of a smooth, 200m concrete loop.

This was where I was going to demonstrate my ability as a real ultra-runner. I had been lapping so consistently, so steadily, like a machine – lap after lap after lap. Poetry in motion indeed. Shuffling

Going well in the early stages of the Brno Indoor 48-hour race in 2004, before the "wheels came off"!

around, feet almost silent on the slippery surface with minimal leg lift. The race was 12 hours old and I was feeling like I could run for ever.

It happened so suddenly. I couldn't believe it. My stomach suddenly cramped. It felt like it was turning inside out. I'd had no warning, no inkling that something was wrong or going wrong. I had no time to do anything, to make a correction in my meticulously researched nutritional plan – everything was planned and written down. My helper, Petra, a quiet, patient, local schoolgirl, had almost learned it by heart.

I slowed dramatically; I clutched my stomach. Next a massive wave of nausea came over me, I struggled to stay upright, I just managed to wobble round to my pit area. I snatched at the nearest bowl and emptied my guts into it, in one huge vomit. My throat and nostrils burnt as the stomach acid did its work. The look on Petra's face said it all. My senses were swimming and I sat with my head between my knees as waves of nausea and more vomiting followed.

Stomach problems and vomiting when racing had bedevilled me during the previous eight years but nothing like this. I had received expert sports nutrition advice over that time, tried numerous diets and eating regimes, but here I was floored, stunned and unbelieving.

Petra, unbeknownst to me, had been so alarmed by my ashen pallor that she had alerted the race doctor. A large gentleman with a huge moustache and ruddy cheeks. I was initially annoyed but she had done the right thing and I later thanked her. He was soon bending over me. Questions followed. He sounded my chest. More questions were fired at me. He said I could stay in the race but insisted on a very long break. It was wise advice and I was in no position to do otherwise.

To cut a long story short, I rested and slept for many hours. I awakened feeling better but somewhat chastened. What now? It was a 48 hour race so runners and walkers were still relentlessly lapping around me. There was another day to go. There was nothing for it, I would return to the fray and I did! Albeit I walked the entire second day, with my tail between my legs - defeated.

The aim in these fixed time events is to cover as much distance as possible in the allotted time. It's up to you whether you walk, run or take a break. It's a fascinating challenge of athleticism, fatigue and time management.

My ego was taking a real bashing. I was at rock bottom. I had plenty of time to think – maybe too much time. I was a champion at shorter races but believed I had more to offer at longer races. Yet, here I was, walking lap after dreary lap feeling totally defeated. Other runners offered support – a helpful tip, a word of encouragement, a pat on the shoulder – but I knew it was all over for this race. I felt embarrassed, weak and lost. I had to face going home empty handed. How would I answer all the friendly "Well, how did you get on?" enquiries. I had a lot of quiet support from Orkney's close-knit communities.

I thought about my appetite for performance. My enthusiasm and proven ability for ultra-distance running. I was determined to sort out my stomach issues, as I believed I had so much more to achieve in this sport and wanted to tackle even longer distances. I wasn't throwing in the towel just yet but others thought differently. A potential member of my support team back in the UK was told by a prominent athlete "you're wasting your time with him!"

Brno was my 43rd ultra-marathon and just my second 48 hour race. Why was I looking to run even further? It always came back to personal curiosity - that was always the answer. When first asking about ultra-races in 1993 I queried "How long are they? The whimsical answer came back "they are as long as your imagination!"

I had a vivid imagination but the issue was that my stomach wasn't cooperating and this was seriously hampering me from truly assessing my ability for running longer.

As I I relentlessly walked those laps in Brno I watched what other runners were doing, how they were eating and drinking. I was looking for answers, looking for ideas. I was after all the 'new boy' at these longer events.

The coach journey back to Prague was a long 205 kilometres, followed by a flight to Gatwick and then towards more northerly latitudes and home. I remember emerging into Gatwick Airport feeling at absolutely rock-bottom. "Where now", I thought. I phoned a friend to share my desperation and seek reassurance and suggestions. They thought my drinks had been too strong and suggested I try more dilute ones. I knew the journey back from this low point was going to be a long and rocky one.

Once back in the peace and quiet of Sanday, I walked the windswept shores and marvelled at the amazing beaches, the bird life, the fresh air, the isolation and the solitude. My thoughts began to clear and I had an epiphany – it is now all up to me, it has to be!

No one knew my strengths, my weaknesses, my talent and my level of desire better than me. I was 51 years old and I realised that I had been listening too closely to the advice of others, particularly on diet and nutrition. The best expert on William Sichel was William Sichel, I had to take charge of my own running destiny.

0-0-0-0

Three years later I would return to this event to take fifth place overall and second in my age

Category, with a Scottish record distance of 213.92 miles.

Early years and table tennis

... 'I wanted to be world class' ...

Aged three in Welford.

West End, Welford – my home until I was ten.

I was born in the Northamptonshire village of Welford in October, 1953, the second son and fifth surviving child, of Dr Gerald Robert McKenzie and Betty Page Sichel.

Welford, with a population of about 1,000, is located on the River Avon border with Leicestershire. Being halfway between Northampton and Leicester, Welford was formerly an important stagecoach stop. Nowadays, it's often known for being signposted off the M1.

Dad was the local GP and his practice covered a wide, rural area, including the village. Our large doctor's house at West End included a dispensary, surgery, and waiting room as well as extensive outbuildings, a very large garden, a tennis court, and an enclosed area of rough ground where Dad

kept some wild rabbits for use while training his gun dogs.

Going with Dad to 'shoots' is a lasting memory and not a very fond one – noisy, cold, wet, with a lot of dead animals and birds, it didn't seem to be my idea of fun even at that young age.

At home, the phone was always ringing and Mum, as the dutiful doctor's wife, did most of the answering. Although Dad was part of a medical practice, under the new National Health Service, he was essentially working alone and was always, it seemed, on-call, frequently heading off in the dead of night to outlying small villages and farms way out in the countryside.

My early life was one surrounded by a lot of other children, especially girls – the family steadily expanded until there were nine of us – five girls and four boys and I was plumb in the middle.

With effectively one generation covering the whole family, my oldest sister Barbara was almost like a second mother-figure and very much so to Rachel, the youngest. Each of us had a different experience of growing up, depending on where we were placed in the family. In later life, it was always a bit of a joke that the first three girls, Barbara, Jenny, and Ruth had the 'life of Riley", with private

Cricket in the garden in Welford with Dad and older brother
Johnny giving advice.

schools, ponies and, a tennis court. Then, as the head count gradually increased, first the private schools went, then the ponies and finally the tennis court.

By the time I came along, life was more normal in that respect although we did have domestic staff to help Mum in the kitchen and run a very large household and GP practice. Mrs Pearsall, who worked in the kitchen, became very much one of the family as we all grew up with her. When we moved south in 1963, it was a huge wrench saying goodbye.

A typical, small mixed farm lay exactly opposite where we lived in West End and from a very young age I loved to go over to Farmer Brown to help with the farmwork. He was very amenable and basically let me join in with everything. From the age of six or seven, I was allowed to handle one teat when the house cow was milked every day.

They didn't have a tractor - a horse and trap was the means of transport around the farm and he let me take the reins at every opportunity. When going through gates I remember being terrified that we would collide with the gate posts, but I needn't have worried, the horse always seemed to know what it was doing – I didn't realise it, but I was superfluous.

My friend Michael Gardiner's parents ran a large dairy farm, The Glebe, just outside Welford, and I was a regular visitor there too, especially at weekends and in the long school holidays. I loved working with Michael on the farm, helping with everything, from the daily chores of milking, which was all done by machine there, to working in the hay during the summer. Sometimes we just kicked around as lads do. It was to The Glebe I would return, for long summer holidays, for a few years after we left Welford.

While I loved life in Welford, the freedom, the farm work and the small school, Mum found that being a doctor's wife in a small but busy practice wasn't so nice. She wanted Dad to leave general practice so that we could have a more normal life without the continuous interruptions which went with a family doctor's duties.

You can imagine my horror when we were all informed that Dad had accepted a job with the Ministry of Health in London and we would all be moving south to Ryarsh in Kent. I was just approaching my tenth birthday. I can't honestly remember how the others reacted, although I understand that my older sisters were delighted as Welford was too quiet for them. I was devastated. I was living the rural dream, although I didn't know it at the time and this would all be coming to an end.

The move to Ryarsh, near West Malling in Kent, was completed during the school holidays of 1963 in an attempt to lessen the impact of the move on the children. Starting new schools was a major ordeal and one not experienced by any of us.

I found it particularly traumatic being very small and very shy yet always one of the oldest in the class thanks to my October birthday. Starting new schools was an unwanted experience that was to happen all too frequently in the coming years.

An early experience was of groups of children coming up to me in the playground and asking me to say 'record', then running away laughing. This I found bizarre so went home and mentioned it to Mum who explained that I had a weak 'r' and my responses amused the local children. School playgrounds can be cruel places.

With the move south, the gun dogs remained in Welford, presumably re-homed and with a much smaller house in Ryarsh, our choice of animal was much reduced. We were, however, allowed to keep some pet rabbits, which was the start of a lifelong interest in rabbit-keeping which endured for another 40 years.

We didn't have the same level of freedom in Ryarsh but I soon made contact with a local dairy farmer, Mr Goodwin and in no time at all I started doing the milk round with him every Saturday morning.

Looking back, I can see that I had a very active childhood, always walking and cycling everywhere. We had no television and I developed a lifelong love of radio listening that I still enjoy today.

Another job for Dad was always in the offing, so it came as no real surprise when we were told that we were once again on the move, this time to Tonbridge in Kent. I dreaded the thought of another new school but obviously had to just get on with it.

The house in Tonbridge was a large three-story building with outbuildings and a large garden.

We all had sufficient space, although bedrooms were always shared with at the very least one other sibling and usually two. One of the outbuildings had room for a cut-down-sized snooker table and a wooden cover which made an excellent, if somewhat small, table tennis table. This provided us with hours of fun.

When I moved up a year at my new school, Slade Primary, my education came to a standstill for

Enthusiastically watching the school sports in Welford.

some years. My new class teacher had a fearsome reputation, long before I knew I was to be his pupil and this resulted in many sleepless nights during the summer holidays preceding the new term.

I dreaded every day at school now and was literally paralysed, educationally, because of my fear of the teacher. His 'party piece' was to stand miscreants on a desk in front of the whole class and whack the backs of their calves with a ruler. Sounds rather tame nowadays but this humiliation was dreaded by me.

I pleaded with Mum and Dad to speak to the headteacher and to try and alleviate my distress, but they were very reluctant to do so and never did anything.

Some solace was found in the physical education lessons, which I loved and seemed to excel at from a young age. I learned to walk on my hands and once garnered a hatful of house points for walking the width of the gym on my hands in front of the whole school. Perhaps that was my first sporting success?

The 'eleven plus' exam, which would decide my next school, secondary or grammar, came and went without success. It was all double Dutch to me, as I seemed to be at a standstill with my schooling.

My first secondary modern school was the Hugh Christie in Tonbridge. I started there in September, 1967, in a smart new uniform and was very glad to have left the Slade Primary.

I performed perfectly well in class and was happily mid-stream but my best memories of Hugh Christie come from the games field. The school had a passionate Welsh rugby teacher

Rugby was the first sport where I had proper coaching. In this faded photograph, I am seen in my familiar scrum half position.

who introduced me to rugby for the first time. I enjoyed it a lot and rugby became my sport for the next five years or so. This was my first experience of organised sports coaching and training and I loved it.

In 1967, we moved to Sevenoaks and yet another new school, Wilderness Secondary Modern, which was a convenient 10-minute walk from home which kept me fit and active as I went home for lunch too.

After the end of year exams in 1969, my Dad received a letter from the headmaster requesting that he and I go to see him. We were completely mystified. Dad asked me if anything had happened at school to which I replied "no". We just couldn't think of any reason why we might be hauled in to see the Head.

We duly fulfilled our appointment and were absolutely stunned to be told that I had come top of the school in every subject. In earlier years, there had been a '14 plus' exam which tended to pick up late developers like myself who had failed the '11 plus' exam, but that had been abolished before my time. The Wilderness headmaster was one of the few who was willing to transfer pupils who excelled at this age.

We decided that I would accept the offer of a place at the Tunbridge Wells School from the following September but I found the adjustment to my sixth and final school difficult: getting there involved a long and convoluted one-hour journey; joining a new year of boys, most of whom already knew each other; coupled with my small stature, lack of physical maturity, and extreme shyness.

Despite my slow physical development, I was good on the sportsfield. It was at about this time, my early teens, that I first formulated the idea that I wanted to be 'world class' at a sport, without knowing which sport. I think I was heavily influenced and possibly inspired, by a general sports magazine around at that time called *World Sports*. There, I read about the training and success of table tennis players, fencers, rowers, weightlifters, and so on. This must have pricked my imagination and somehow fired me up to want to become a sporting success.

I started training on my own, at weekends, for the first time, running from my home in Bayham Road, Sevenoaks, up to Godden Green and back, a distance of perhaps a couple of miles. I enjoyed it and it was a start. Even in those days, I revelled in the post-exercise sensations of euphoria and that feeling of being tired but fit. I think also that training and sport really boosted my self-esteem which was vital for me, especially when having to cope with so many new schools.

I continued with my interest in rugby and represented Tunbridge Wells School for some years as scrum-half. I never enjoyed the off-pitch gregariousness involved with rugby, probably because for me puberty was very late in arriving. The rugby songs on the buses to away matches, the communal showers and so on simply wasn't my thing, but I enjoyed the training and the matches. I gradually realised that all the other players seemed to be getting larger and larger while I stayed the same. It was time to move on to other sporting interests.

My main sporting involvement out of school at this time was table tennis. Our local church, St John's, Sevenoaks, had a vibrant youth club and table tennis was one of the main games played there.

I found that I was quite good at it and enjoyed playing. It was when I beat my older brother, Johnny, in the club tournament that it became my sport of choice.

I joined a local club in the nearby village of Otford and also established a connection with a thriving table tennis centre on the Downham Estate in southeast London, near Bromley. I used to go and practise every week at the Otford Club and was always fascinated by the skills and experience of a veteran player called Sheila. She was hunched and had severe arthritis in her hands but was incredibly difficult to beat. She knew every angle, every trick and made the utmost use of every facility she had left to maximise her performance. She saw off many a young 'buck' but my fitness, enthusiasm and developing skills finally beat her after many a long month of failure.

Table tennis became my first serious sporting passion. I wanted to become 'world class' at it and planned to start in all seriousness after I did a travelling gap year when I left school. During the winter of 1972 I attended a weekly circuit training class in Dulwich, south London. It was organised by England table tennis team coach Les Gresswell, with whom I became very friendly, and he arranged for me to attend the Yugoslav team's 1973 World Table Tennis Championships training camp in Sarajevo, as an observer, prior to that event. This was a precious and unique opportunity for me.

During my six week stay in the capital of Bosnia Herzegovina, I was given unfettered access to the national team in their final build up to a home World Championships. I attended all the training sessions in Skenderija – the 6,000 seater stadium - as the only observer and took copious notes of everything I witnessed. I wrote up my notes, long hand, at night. The tournament was a great success and I attended every day, supporting my Yugoslav heroes as they achieved medals in men's singles and doubles.

When I got back to the UK I took up a place at Chelsea College, London University, to study Human Biology. I was in Halls of Residence, just a few steps from the King's Road, the mecca of popular culture and the swinging 60s, which I had just missed, but I had little interest in pop music, girls or drinking. I was totally focused on my table tennis, my studies and thought of myself very much as a non-conformist.

I was enrolled on to the three year Human Biology course which was the nearest I could get to [what is now known as] Sports Science, as it had a number of physiology units included in it. I worked hard, especially in the early morning, often having already studied for a couple of hours and been for a run in Battersea Park before lectures at 9am.

My life for much of the next seven years revolved around St Brides Table Tennis Centre at Ludgate Circus, near St Paul's Cathedral, where I practised for countless hours with a variety of players, including Geoff Golding. I didn't actually play games with Geoff but practised stroke play endlessly and my outstanding endurance started to become evident. He would defend relentlessly while I would attack with my powerful forehand loop shot across the diagonals. I grooved an immensely strong and consistent stroke that became world class.

At weekends I often travelled to tournaments around the UK, especially in the north of England. The journeys there and back by train were usually long and tedious. I would arrive at my destination on a Friday night and only get back to London late on Sunday night, with lectures at 9am the next day. My results were often disappointing but in Bradford I achieved my best ever result, beating England's No 10 ranked player, Nigel Eckersley.

One of the things I liked to do, in this period, was to test myself both physically and mentally. I might practise for a number of exhausting hours with Geoff down at the St Bride's Club and, after returning to my room, would ask myself "Am I really that tired?" To answer that question, I would then set off to the Barnet Table Tennis Centre, in north London, and practise all evening there, before returning home late at night. Clearly, the 'feeling of being tired' was very different from actually being exhausted. I had proved to myself that tiredness was, more often than not, more mental than physical.

I was an extremely enthusiastic, hard working and determined table tennis player. I was prepared to travel to the ends of the earth to give myself the chance of achieving my goal and becoming 'world class'.

I had two idols in sport. In the sport of squash, there was Jonah Barrington. He considered himself not very talented but had an incredible work ethic and devoted himself to physical fitness so that he could wear down players considered more talented but less fit.

I also had the Yugoslav Table Tennis Champion, Dragutin Surbek, as a role model. His fitness and attacking style really excited me. I too devoted myself to physical training to make sure I never lost due to lack of fitness. I ran daily and attended physical training sessions whenever I could. I used the Chelsea College gym hall to do shuttle runs. I would do a physical warm up before matches, which was unheard of in those days. I garnered the nickname 'Superman' and was thought of as a fitness fanatic.

In practice, it seemed that I could beat anyone, but in competitive games I frequently under performed. I often lost in the first round to an unknown player, not having been able to get my best shots in. I was tight in matches. I couldn't relax and release my talent like I did in training. It was all inexplicable to me and dreadfully embarrassing and disappointing. I felt I was letting people down. I didn't like matches and competition. I preferred training and practice – I was a 'training champion'.

A well-known player and promoter once said rather cruelly "Bill [as Londoners preferred to call me] is world class until the umpire says 'love all'" – sadly, he was right.

But what to do about it? Back in the 1970s, I had never heard of sports psychology. I don't think it even existed then. I can see now that the knowledge and experience that I needed just wasn't around then and my peer group were equally mystified with my inability to realise my true potential.

One day in 1976, a young Japanese business man, with minimal English, named Taku Fujioka, walked down the dingy steps into the St Bride's Centre and asked for a game. He became a regular in the basement club and picked up on my ambition and enthusiasm.

To my surprise and delight, he asked if I would like to train in Japan? At that time, the Japanese were the second best in the world at table tennis. I nearly bit his hand off. Of course, yes, I would love to, but how could it possibly happen. I had just graduated with a BSc (Hons) Upper Second degree. I had been offered the chance to do a PhD but turned it down. I also passed on the degree presentation by the Queen Mother. That non-conformist in me was coming out again. I now had a part-time job as a domestic at Imperial College. This funded my cost of living and my table tennis travel in the UK – but not to Japan!

In order to make this dream opportunity become reality, I went to live and work in Holland, where I earned good money in a paper factory. I had a tenuous connection with a former England player, Judy Williams, who lived in Amsterdam and had a spare room for me. She introduced me to table tennis contacts and I subsequently met the bullish and eccentric coach, Nigerian Dutchman Jolley Sojinu. He was to figure largely in my final years as a player and I am still in contact with him to this day.

I saved money and in December, 1977, I was en route to Japan. My first experience of a long-haul flight saw me leaving Heathrow and travelling over Alaska before breaking my journey in Seoul, South Korea. I then continued on to a hot and humid Haneda Airport in Tokyo – my home for the next six months. It turned out that Taku was an Old Boy of the Nihon (Japan) University in Tokyo and still had many connections there in the table tennis community.

Recognised sports people in Japan can get preferential access to university places by virtue of their expertise in a range of different sports. The students lived together in club houses, with others training in the same sport. I was fortunate enough to have been granted a place in the Nihon University Table Tennis Club House in downtown Tokyo, on the Odakyu train line.

I trained hard in Japan and came to love living there. I travelled the length of the country with fellow students and coaches. I competed in the All-Japan National Championships but my mental weaknesses continued to dog me in competition. I led the champion from Hiroshima by 20 points to 13 in the deciding game. I needed just one more point to seal my victory. I lost! My coach was dumbfounded. I felt ashamed and embarrassed.

Playing the Hiroshima champion in the 1977 All-Japan Championships in the Olympic Stadium in Tokyo. I lost despite a huge lead of 20-13 in one game.

I arrived back home just before Christmas, in 1977. Coming home was a huge and unexpected culture shock for which I was totally unprepared. I had become so adapted to Japanese life. I had given up my part-time work in London, so I had no job. Similarly, I had vacated my room in London too, so I had to go and live at home in Sevenoaks. It was a difficult time for me.

In my sports life I was at a high point but there was simply nowhere to go and continue such a lifestyle in the UK. The table tennis training facility I had in

Japan simply didn't exist anywhere in the UK in those days.

I soon returned to London, got another part-time job as a book-keeper, rented a room in North London and returned to my old haunts at St Bride's. It was all a bit of a comedown to be honest and I was unable to fully capitalise on my Japanese training.

There was a high point in 1978 when I was employed for a couple of weeks, as a practice partner and translator for Mitsuru Kohno, the 1977 World Table Tennis Champion. I toured venues across the country with him and it was an amazing experience for me.

In 1978 I landed a 'dream' job for two weeks, as interpreter and practice partner for the world champion, Mitsuro Kohno from Japan. He was doing a tour of exhibition matches throughout England.

It was difficult to know how to progress my table tennis career from that point. There was no money in the game in the UK. Professional leagues were starting in Europe, particularly in Germany and Holland. I wanted to play and compete with the best.

I decided to activate my Scottish heritage – my father was born in Glasgow – and become an Anglo-Scot for table tennis purposes. From then on, I regularly commuted between London and the leading clubs in Edinburgh and Glasgow. This

In April, 1980 I was part of the Scottish squad that attended the European Table Tennis Championships in Berne, Switzerland. I'm second left.

worked out well and I managed to reach the semi-finals of the Scottish Championships. This led to me being in the Scottish squad that travelled to the European Table Tennis Championship in Bern, Switzerland, in 1980. I also represented Scotland in the West German Championships, along with an up and coming player called David Hannah.

Despite this modest success, I was still under performing in competition, dogged by nerves and stage fright. In matches I wasn't able to play my best. I didn't have enough self-confidence to control a game, or a tactical brain that would allow me to engineer openings for my strongest shots. Looking back now, I can see that I just didn't like competitions. I didn't feel comfortable with the idea of trying to beat someone.

Following the Swiss European tournament, I was

able to take up another unique opportunity. This time I had managed to organise a training trip to Beijing in China. It came about after conversations with the Chinese team's translator when they were playing in a tournament in the UK. To go to China, in any capacity, at that time was extremely unusual but the establishment of diplomatic relations with the USA in 1979 – known as President Nixon's 'ping pong diplomacy' - led to a relaxation of controls allowing some tourism to start.

I spent four weeks in July, training at the Beijing Institute of Physical Culture. Myself and my companion, Malcolm Francis, were housed in the 'foreigners accommodation block' away from our coach, training partner and translator. It was very basic and had no air conditioning but we did have a Belgian chef and European-style meals were served.

My training partner in Beijing, Guo Chung Pei.

My coach in Beijing, Li Shou Tung.

This was a punishing training experience in the heat and humidity of a Chinese summer. Even then, I was extremely conscientious about preparation and I had rigorously heat acclimatised by submersing myself in hot baths while monitoring my body temperature. It sounds funny but it worked and turned out to be essential. Because of my meticulous preparation, I was able to take full advantage of this training opportunity.

As had happened in the past, the experienced Chinese coach was impressed with my practising abilities but baffled by my inability to utilise my skills in competitive games. Nevertheless, when I returned from China, I thought that I was playing my best ever. I had thrived under the one-to-one coaching and the long hours of rigorous training.

Since working in Holland, I had maintained my contact with coach Jolley Sojinu and he suggested that I should move to Holland for part-time work, intensive practice and a semi-professional contract with a second division team called 'The Salamanders' in The Hague. This appeared to be a good option for me.

It was the end of August, 1980, and within a couple of days of returning to London from Beijing I was on a ferry to Europe and a train up to Leiden for a new life in Holland.

To cut a long story short, things just didn't work out for me in Holland. I managed to get enough part-time work and I also got suitable accommodation sorted out but finding sufficient practice partners proved to be a stumbling block. Playing for De

Multi-ball training with Li Shou Tung, using their favoured multi-ball practice method.

Salamanders Club in The Hague was disheartening as the petty competitiveness and gamesmanship of my opponents was a far cry from the level of competition I sought. When Jolley suggested I work full-time, I knew that this set-up wasn't going to meet my expectations.

February arrived and I made a sudden decision to retire from table tennis.

It was a very distressing decision to make but I knew that the time was right. I had come to the end of the road in so many ways. I was gutted. All my sporting dreams were going up in smoke. I was lost and bereft.

Jolley simply couldn't come to terms with my radical decision. He thought I would rapidly re-consider and then resume training. He came round to my flat often, pleading with me to return to training. His pleas fell on deaf ears - my decision was final and I never resumed training. I seemed to know when it was time for a major change and this would be repeated throughout my life.

Looking back now, 40 years later, I can see that I was like a square peg in a round hole. I was ahead of my time and I was never able to find the right set up for what I wanted to do. I was on a high returning from China but was never able to capitalise on it. There may have been a suitable club set-up for me, somewhere, but I wasn't aware of anything and I couldn't Google it, like I would now!

In researching this book, I had a long conversation with Melvyn Waldman, a former England Junior International player and he thought it was odd that I had crumbled in competition as a table tennis player. He wondered if it was because I was facing my opponent, just nine feet away, staring them in the face. If you are nervous and lacking in confidence, this can be quite off-putting, a stare can feel aggressive and intimidating.

Partnership in Orkney

… 'we had a lot in common' …

Once I had made the dramatic and sudden decision in Holland to retire from table tennis, the next thing was - what now?

I had run for about 20 minutes a day as part of my training regime for table tennis and I had always known that I was quite good at it. This had become apparent at a table tennis training camp in Slovenia a few years earlier. The Slovene trainer was furious with the squad and thought that some squad members weren't training hard enough. He organised a 'punishment run', uphill and down dale for a distance of about five miles. I loved it and won it by miles. All the others were complaining and swearing about it and trying to get lifts to the finish.

I had banked that experience and now I decided that I was going to put my energies into running. I was going to run a marathon.

In 1981, there was a marathon boom sweeping through the United States and it was coming over to Europe. This marathon craze was so successful that over the next few years there was hardly a major town or city anywhere that didn't have its marathon.

I started getting the latest running magazines and learning about different types of training for distance running. I joined a local Dutch athletics club but always felt an outsider. I did a few local races quite satisfactorily but I was incredibly naive about the sport.

I travelled back to England in May, 1981, and stayed with one of my five sisters as she lived relatively close to the Birmingham People's Marathon route in Solihull. I always remember being quite intimidated when walking to the start line because an old guy next to me said he had done a marathon every weekend of the year so far!

I finished my first marathon in 54th place, with 2 hours 43 minutes 49 seconds. My first thought was "Blast it – I'm half an hour off the World Record!" It was only many years later that my reaction was somewhat different, being amazed at what I had done on so little training and less than three months as a runner.

I continued to work in Holland while I contemplated my future and enjoyed my distance running. I did various jobs, including cleaner in a block of student flats. The students all came from conservative families and they couldn't understand how I could be happy in my job when I already had the university qualifications for which they strived.

Regarding my future, my main conclusion was that I had been happiest when living in Welford and living in a small, agricultural community in a rural environment. I then determined that I would try and head in that direction again. The difficulty was in trying to interpret that into my current context.

I joined various Dutch organisations that were interested in sustainable living, smallholding and small scale wind power generation. I spent a lot of time in the local library in Leiden and looked into the possibility of moving into various rural communities in Holland but I was heavily warned off this idea and told that outsiders wouldn't be welcomed. I also looked into the cost of buying a small plot of land in Holland but the prices were exorbitant.

I then started studying the UK property sections of a publication called *Exchange and Mart* and I soon noticed that the further north one went, the cheaper the properties got. Hence, as I had limited funds, I started examining more closely the sections covering northern Scotland, the Western Isles, Orkney and Shetland. I came across adverts for 'crofts' for the first time and then read extensively about crofting in Scotland.

Orkney became my focus of attention and the more I read about the islands, the more interested I became. I started a long corresponding with Paul Davidson, from the Department of Agriculture in Kirkwall and learned about the farming economy in Orkney and the possibilities for income from a small croft. I knew that because of my meagre savings, I would have to buy or rent something small and probably derelict too, but I was prepared for that eventuality.

I had invested a lot of time investigating small scale wind turbines, as I had assumed that I wouldn't have mains power. I even went so far as to have some small parts made for me in Holland, that would allow small blades to be attached to a car alternator, which could then generate 12-volt electricity.

Early in 1982, I decided that I would travel to Orkney in May, for a month, to have a good look around and see what I thought. I placed an advert in *The Orcadian* newspaper for a small, cheap, croft and I got one reply.

Meanwhile, in Kent, my brother Johnny announced that he was getting married in February and I travelled from Leiden for the wedding and used the opportunity to catch up with my huge family.

I was sitting at home, in the kitchen, explaining to my mum and youngest sister Rachel about my plans to visit Orkney in May, when Rachel piped up that she thought the lady next door to where she looked after a friend's horses also wanted to go to Orkney.

"What?" I screeched, "I want to go and meet her". Moving to Orkney was pretty outlandish and unusual in the early 1980s and to find someone else who wanted to go there too was a chance too good to miss.

Rachel wasn't too keen as she said she didn't know the lady that well and how would she introduce me? I insisted and that afternoon we went out to the village of Sevenoaks Weald and I was introduced to Elizabeth Austen.

When we knocked on the cottage door, a fearsome barking ensued, but soon Elizabeth appeared and Ben, the dog, was told to be quiet – his bark was worse than his bite, thank goodness. I was led into the freezing cottage and Rachel left me to talk about Orkney with Elizabeth.

I walked with Elizabeth through the local woods to bring her goats home, collecting twigs and branches for the fire as we went. I sipped some cold goats' milk indoors, but never got a cup of tea – Elizabeth later explained that she didn't light the fire until evening time.

It came to light that she had made a flying visit to Orkney earlier that month and had bought a derelict, roofless croft called Upper Breckan, along with ten acres of surrounding land. It was on one of Orkney's Northern Isles, Sanday. She planned to live in a small caravan on site until she had made the ruin habitable and then move in. Other plans were fairly vague.

When I first met Elizabeth in February, 1982, in Weald in Kent, she showed me this picture of Upper Breckan, Sanday and said "I've bought this!"

Elizabeth (39) had never married, had no family and was an early retired nurse, due to a bad back. She had taken up country living out in the sticks near Sevenoaks, in preparation for a more permanent move to a small holding of her own.

Some time later, Rachel came to look for me - we were still talking about Orkney and Elizabeth's plans. We had a lot in common.

I went ahead with my planned visit to Orkney Mainland in May and for the final week I travelled to Sanday, accepting Elizabeth's invitation to spend

There are the most wonderful skyscapes in Sanday. This one looks across Roos Loch in Burness.

The sunsets in Sanday can be spectacular. This one is at Cata Sands.

time there before I returned to Holland. It was a very hard-working holiday as I laboured long hours in the bright spring weather to dig a latrine and establish a large vegetable garden for Elizabeth.

I saw how stunningly beautiful the island was with the green fields carpeted in bright yellow dandelions. The beaches were just miles of golden sands and the clear blue skies and long hours of daylight lent an alluring sense of magic to the place.

It's difficult to portray how remote her croft was and how few amenities she had – basically nothing at all. No water supply, no electricity, no phone – zilch. I was also very well aware that Elizabeth was at a very low ebb, having really struggled in her first six weeks in Sanday. There was late snow, which she hadn't been expecting, a treasured goat had died and the cost of heating her flimsy ill-equipped

Whitemill Bay, Sanday.

caravan was alarmingly high. It became a bit of a joke that with my arrival the skies cleared and the sun shone around the clock!

From my point of view, I liked the edgy feel of Sanday, Elizabeth and I got on well and I wanted a hard life but felt that doing it by myself might be a step too far. At that moment in time this seemed like the place to be and I felt that we could make a go of things together. So, after knowing Elizabeth for just a week, I asked her if she would consider sharing the croft? I thought she would need to think it over but no, not Elizabeth, she immediately responded enthusiastically "that's a great idea, you can have one end and I'll have the other!" So the deal was done, with oddly, no mention of money.

This was the picture I took in July, 1982 when I arrived to live in Sanday. It shows the caravan we lived in until September.

Elizabeth in her trademark orange Crocs.

I also made it clear to Elizabeth that my sporting days were most definitely over. Elizabeth wasn't interested in sport whatsoever, although she was a good walker and she was relieved to hear that I wouldn't be heading away anytime soon in pursuit of more sporting challenges.

I returned to Leiden and over the next few weeks I packed up my room, finished my job and on one July day, my former coach and now friend, Jolley, saw me off from the local bus station for my long trek and my new life in Sanday.

It was mid-day on July 19, 1982, and I had just arrived at Upper Breckan when the neighbours, crofters Jock and Isa Muir, came over to explain that they were getting their hay bales in and could we lend a hand? This resulted in us spending the whole day carting small square bales on a hot summer's afternoon. We met the extended family and finished up with a huge supper and some of Jock's home brew. I wasn't a drinker, so I had to almost crawl the 150m to Elizabeth's caravan to finally crash out.

Sitting here in Kirkwall, in the summer of 2021, it's very hard to capture that sense of isolation we experienced in our early years in Sanday, with no telephone landline (mobiles and the internet weren't yet invented) and the nearest telephone box was three-quarters of a mile up the road.

Post was very slow, taking days either way and the shipping service was a three-days-a-week affair and two day returns a year – the Annual Trip Day and the Orkney Agricultural Show Day, which, for many years, was my only day off!

Elizabeth was a good letter writer and kept up with a pen friend in New Zealand and I would keep in contact with my old table tennis friend, Geoff. We would arrange a date and time for the next call and I would usually cycle up for the next pre-arranged chat. To my amazement, he eventually moved with his family from Kent to retire in Sanday. They stayed for many years before eventually moving down to the Scottish Borders. Similarly, I would phone my parents at regular intervals from the old phone box.

We both found the pace of life in Sanday very slow, especially in the early days when we had so much to do and were often racing against time to get things done and get things started. In many ways, the fact that so many people had time to speak, that islanders had time for each other, that travel took a long time, that most people had plenty of time for social events and so on was a very good and healthy thing.

It was just that we were starting from the very bare bones of existence, building up the ruin, developing a kitchen garden, trying to start a business and trying to get basic shelter before the winter gales set in.

I celebrate the roof going on in September, 1982. Elizabeth's dog, Ben, is in the foreground.

It's interesting to wonder what effect the social and physical isolation had on our personal relationship and business decisions. Luckily, Elizabeth and I were at the same time best friends as well as partners and that stood us in good stead during our 35 years together. We also had three things in our favour, which allowed our unlikely relationship to prosper. We had both been used to living on a very low income. We both had a very strong desire to get established in Sanday and to make a life there and finally, we had no bolt hole – there was no convenient house somewhere 'down south' where we could retreat if it all ended in failure. We had to succeed.

To kick things off on the right foot, we got married on December 21, 1982, a little over five months since I joined her in Sanday.

Me and Elizabeth in the back garden looking out towards North Ronaldsay in 1983. (Picture: Thomas van Nes).

long fronds of laminaria seaweed that get thrown up on to the beach during the winter storms. We contacted the local tangle agent and, sadly for us, there was to be no tangle-gathering that year

December 21st 1982 – Elizabeth and I got married in Lettan, in the North End of Sanday.

Our first ten years in Orkney were the toughest years of my life as we struggled beyond belief to get established and generate a reliable income. Our range of options was severely limited. We had savings between us but not a lot and we were extremely reluctant to borrow as neither of us had been in debt before.

The initial plan had been to work in the local 'tangle' industry. This involved working on exposed beaches during the winter months, gathering the

Milking time in 1983. (Picture: Thomas van Nes).

Hay making with a friend in 1983. (Picture: Thomas van Nes).

Busy with my old petrol/paraffin, 'Grey Fergie' in 1983.
(Picture: Thomas van Nes).

due to a lack of world demand for the alginates they contained. This came as a huge blow to our plans, as a key part of our planned income had been wiped out at a stroke.

We were thrown into desperation. I avidly researched a range of small business opportunities that might work on our small holding, but it was tough. Postal enquiries seemed to take weeks and we had so little to start with that our opportunities were very limited.

Eventually, I decided that we should go into farmed rabbit meat production. Islanders had lived on wild rabbit during the war years and

In 1987 I was a "Venturecash Initiative" award winner.
I'm photographed at the final presentations held at the
Grosvenor Hotel in Edinburgh.

beyond but stopped eating it in the 1950s due to the outbreak of myxomatosis. I filled our recently vacated caravan with home-made rabbit hutches constructed from dis-used furniture. Initial stock came from Aberdeenshire and we got under way.

We did a pilot project for about a year and then we managed to secure a small grant and loan from the Highlands and Islands Development Board. This enabled us to build a substantial rabbit unit, potentially housing hundreds of rabbits. We grew our own feed to keep costs down and ran this business for a few years, overcoming many setbacks and difficulties along the way. We also developed our craft skills by tanning the skins and making a range of products from the rabbit fur.

However, the bottom line was that there was no profit in the business. The cost of feeding the rabbits and the high delivery charges meant that we could only just about break even at best. It had no future.

By great good fortune, in 1987, I managed to be one of four Scottish winners of a farming diversification initiative called Venturecash. My prize was an award of £1,000 and I subsequently learned about angora wool production from one of the other winners. I immediately recognized the suitability and possibilities for us in Sanday and went about securing some initial stock.

To cut a long story short, we immediately started to re-direct our business towards angora production.

Elizabeth was a wonderful and enthusiastic gardener. She developed large areas of flowers, shrubs and a bountiful kitchen garden too.

Upper Breckan, looking towards Scar House.

Elizabeth in full bloom.

Angora wool dyeing became the main business of Orkney Angora.

The transition took time but was successful and gave us hope, which was very important. We had been beaten down by so many setbacks and disappointments but now there was light at the end of the tunnel. Over the coming years, Breckan Rabbits morphed into Breckan Rabbits Craft Centre and finally Orkney Angora. We were able to trade our way out of financial difficulties forever.

Elizabeth in 1986 with the newly arrived Bella and two-year-old Tanya.

Having fun with Tanya in front of the old Welstood stove in 1983. (Picture: Thomas van Nes).

An early family photo from 1988.

We developed a thriving craft shop in the croft, where Elizabeth enjoyed greeting the summer visitors and we grew the angora wool business with both wholesale and retail sales in the UK, Europe and the Far East. At first, this was by means of a traditional mail order format with a printed catalogue but this gradually changed as the internet came along in 1995 and our website replaced the laborious job of producing the catalogues, which we had done entirely in-house.

In 1992, after ten years of intense hard work and stress and strain, getting married, building up the croft, welcoming first Tanya and then Bella into the family and starting up a small business, I started to have a strange feeling that I could only describe as 'needing more'. I was very honest with Elizabeth and said I wasn't going anywhere but I just wanted her to know. Somehow and in some way, I felt my needs were not being met.

With the business having turned the corner into profitability, I also became aware that for the first time since moving to Sanday, I could actually have some time off and perhaps I could return to doing some kind of sport again.

I looked around at what was available on the island and really, at that time, it was only the golf club – Sanday has a nine hole golf course – but that didn't really appeal to me.

It was April 12, 1992, and I sat down at Upper Breckan, turned on the telly and the London Marathon was on. I thought "I could go for a run" ….

Champion and cancer victim

... 'you might be an ultra runner' ...

Two months after I rediscovered running, I was toeing the line at Orkney's premier half marathon which was held in the southern island of Hoy – two ferry trips away from Sanday. I comfortably completed the hilly course in 1 hour 26 minutes 39 seconds, but it was what happened afterwards that had the most impact.

Following the race, I experienced the most incredible 'runner's high'. It was like I was walking on air for most of the following week. I never experienced such an intense feeling ever again. It made me realise that I had really missed my sporting life during the previous ten years. I had now met a few people from the small running community on Mainland Orkney and I continued training with renewed enthusiasm.

I wanted to compete again, so I travelled down to Glasgow in August that year to run in the 1992 Great Scottish Run Half Marathon. This was a mass event and quite overwhelming for me. I had never seen so many runners, of all shapes and sizes, let alone been among them. I felt very shy and self-conscious, not really knowing the procedures before the race started. Where was I supposed to register? Where should I position myself at the start? Not a clue. As a result, I just went right to the back of the whole lot and went from there.

Well, the gun went and I just flew round that 13.1 mile / 21 km course, overtaking about 8,000 runners to finish in 249th place in 1 hour 22 minutes and 52 seconds. I felt a rush of elation as I crossed the line. Now I knew there was 'something there'. Some ability that was worth training and developing and I really enjoyed it.

As a result of that run, I decided to return to marathon running once again, starting with the Black Isle Marathon that same year. An awful day

of torrential rain and high winds saw me battling to 12th place, with 2 hours 53 minute 46 seconds.

The following year, 1993, I endured the excruciating journey down to the London Marathon, which involved a 90 minute ferry journey from Sanday to Kirkwall for an overnight stay. Then a 30 minute bus journey to Stromness to catch the NorthLink ferry to Scrabster, near Thurso, in Caithness, in the far north of the Scottish mainland.

There, I caught a coach to Inverness, the Highland Capital, where I was able to board an overnight bus to London. I crawled off the next morning at Victoria Coach Station and made my way to the London Marathon Expo to register and thence to my accommodation, where I attempted to ready myself for my race the next morning.

I crossed the finishing line on Westminster Bridge in 2 hours 44 minutes 02 seconds and then hopped back on coaches to Glasgow, Inverness and finally Thurso, before then boarding ferries to Stromness and thence to Kirkwall and finally home on the ferry to Sanday. The travelling was exhausting and very time consuming.

Later that year, I managed to drop my time for the 26.2 miles down to 2 hours 39 minutes, producing almost identical times in the Luton and then the Flying Fox Marathon down in Stone, Staffordshire.

By now, I was ordering my running kit by mail order, with the Edinburgh branch of the Run & Become chain being my main supplier. I was still a real newbie to running and racing and the world had moved on since I had initially dabbled in the sport 13 years before. In fact, the sport was enjoying a veritable boom at that time, which has endured to the present day.

The manager, Adrian Stott, was the guy I usually spoke to and he fielded a host of questions from me relating to training, competing and running kit. I'm embarrassed to say that I once asked him what to wear underneath the modern running shorts which came with a built-in brief and were a new design to me!

In one conversation with Adrian, I happened to mention that I wasn't exhausted when doing a marathon in around 2 hours 39 minutes. There was a brief silence the other end, then Adrian replied "so you felt like you could have kept going?". "Yes" I replied. He responded very quickly "You might be an ultra-runner" to which I replied "What do they do?". "Keep going" was his excited retort.

He then explained that ultra-marathon races were anything beyond the marathon distance, with the shortest ones usually being 31 miles / 50 km and going "as long as you can imagine".

Of course, at the time, I had no idea that Adrian was an established ultra-runner himself as well as being a member of the world-wide Sri Chinmoy meditation group that organised running events from two miles up to 1,000 miles in over 40 countries world-wide!

He then suggested that I might be interested in trying the Scottish 100km Championships the following year, in July, 1994. After he said that they were being held in Edinburgh, around the Herriot Watt, Riccarton Campus, I said "I'll give it a go". Famous last words indeed.

I now recall that I had read something about ultra-running the night before that year's London Marathon. A free copy of *Marathon and Beyond* magazine had been included in the 'goodie bag'. The idea seemed so strange to me that I hadn't fully understood what it was all about.

And so, to the Scottish 100 km championship in Edinburgh. It was summer, so the student halls of residence were available to rent and I had made use of that facility so that I was right on the spot for the 7am start. I think the only people I knew were Adrian, who was also the race director and his wife and two daughters, who all worked in the Run & Become shop with him. He had kindly provided

me with a personal helper, John Sneddon, who would hand me my drinks every lap. John was a keen ultra-runner himself, so he wasn't fazed by being asked to stand roadside, for several hours, helping some country bumpkin, down from the isles.

At the start line I felt quite daunted by the whole thing. I was having to cope with a huge step up in race distance, with my longest race to date being the Isle of Man TT 40-miler (64 km) two months previously. I had no idea what I was doing really. I was surrounded by loads of experienced athletes, who clearly had many 100km races under their belts and much longer distances too. I wasn't worried by having to run 30 laps of the campus. In fact, I found it reassuring, as there was no way I could get lost.

Initially, I stayed in the leading pack of runners, as I felt that they must know what they were doing and how fast to run in these early stages. There was a lot of experience around me. Although I was the 'new boy' and felt it, I was used to running six-minute miles in my marathons and I felt that the pace was very slow, even though I knew I had to run well over two marathons – more than I had ever run before. There was some banter in the pack but I didn't take part in it, feeling that I had nothing to say.

We ran the opening laps in a smidgen over 14 minutes for the 2.08 miles / 3.35km distance. John was reassuringly waiting for me at the exact same spot every lap, which was just what I needed. The main entrance area to the Heriot Watt University, comprising a half-square of student buildings including the sports centre and administration offices and a grassy area, formed the hub of the race, with the lap counting tables, refreshment area and medical tent. With each runner's support crew as well, it was a busy scene and provided a sudden burst of activity each time we passed through, to start yet another lap.

After about ten laps I felt the pace drop and I somehow found the confidence to do my own thing and just decided to maintain the previous pace.

This meant that I moved to the front and soon opened up a significant gap on the main pack. I felt that the pace was still very comfortable for me and I was happy to continue lapping consistently under 15 minutes for the two-mile laps. Because of the twists and turns of the course, I was soon out of sight and it felt very strange leading a race for the first time in my life.

I got some quiet encouragement each lap from John, although I suspect that many thought I would soon 'blow up' and regret my decision to maintain a strong pace. Around the 23 mile mark I got a bad 'stitch', which I eased by using a breathing method which involves breathing out as the leg, on the opposite side to the pain, strikes the ground. This worked, but I was left with a pain in the right side of the diaphragm for the remainder of the race.

I passed the first marathon in a little over 3 hours and 31 miles / 50 km in 3 hours 39 minutes. I was still feeling good. I felt buoyed by the fact that I was being chased by everyone else, while always expecting someone to come breezing past me at any minute.

The previous day, I had felt very humbled indeed, meeting some of Scotland's leading ultra-runners in Adrian's shop in the Haymarket area of Edinburgh. Mick Francis and Alan Stewart spoke of their huge weekly, training mileages and I kept very quiet about my meagre 70 miles. This induced feelings of insecurity and lack of preparedness on my behalf. I was very new to this scene and naively felt like I had no chance against them.

In those days, race performance was often thought to be very closely linked to the number of miles run, every week, in training. While this might be a factor, the point is that in a competition, all that matters is who crosses the finish line first. There are no prizes for those who have logged the most training miles!

It was this scenario that was unfolding in Edinburgh that Sunday morning. The feeling of being chased was with me throughout the race. I wasn't looking behind me and I couldn't hear anyone, so I knew

I must be some distance ahead of the chasing runners. Now I was lapping people and supportive grunts emerged as I sped past.

My drinks strategy was simply 150 mls of ten per cent Leppin. That's 100g of carbohydrate powder / one litre of water, every lap. So, I was drinking about 600mls an hour of dilute carbohydrate solution. I'd had my breakfast of two rounds of white bread, honey sandwiches at 5 am that morning. After 4 hours running, I added in one carbohydrate gel, every other lap. This seemed to work fine.

After about 30 miles, I had a really bad patch and slowed somewhat. Adrian suggested I have one 'easy lap' and then really dig in again. I took his advice and managed to maintain pace again albeit a slower one. Still no one had passed me.

Fifty miles in 6 hours 13 minutes came and went. I was completely out of my comfort zone now. In a wilderness of not knowing. What I did know about was the rising tide of pain in my thighs. My lap times had slid down to 18 and then 19 minutes – but still no one had passed me. I really felt I was starting to labour now. I had never run on such painful legs before. There was nothing to do except keep going, until that finish line came into sight.

I found it difficult to comprehend my position – I was in the final stages of the National Championships, in my first 100km race and I was still in the lead. As I had passed through the race HQ area, I could see and sense the excitement and surprise on many faces. Adrian was appearing more frequently, blurting out misunderstood advice and encouragement. His excitement was palpable now. I felt my chest heaving with emotion as I trudged up the long, steep incline towards the end of the 99th lap – and then it happened.

For the first time for nearly eight hours I suddenly heard chasing footsteps and heavy panting coming up behind me. Just at that moment, a gasping Mick Francis surged passed me, face contorted with the effort and moved quickly ahead up the hill. I was unable to respond.

I was stunned. But as I took the left turn towards the HQ area and the lap finish line, I suddenly saw Mick prostrate on the grassy area. He had collapsed in dramatic fashion after passing me.

I felt a surge of adrenaline and sped onward, with renewed energy, starting my final lap having regained the lead. That last lap was almost a minute faster than the previous one, shocked into overdrive by my competitive spirit and fuelled by a hormone rush. Was Mick going to come back at me? Was someone else making a 'do or die' effort to catch me?

They weren't!

In no time, the finishing tape was stretched out in front of me and I crossed it in 8 hours 1 minute and 9 seconds. My quads were killing me. I didn't really know what to do after I had stopped. I was at the same time elated but bewildered. Adrian was beaming.

Winning my debut 100 km race and becoming Scottish champion at the first attempt in July, 1994.

What happened there? I was the Scottish Champion at the first attempt. This wasn't supposed to happen to me. I was the 'nearly guy', the 'training champion', the keen guy that worked hard but buckled in competition. Where did this winner come from?

Coming down from the isles and having been away from top sport for 13 years, I experienced overwhelming feelings of relief and elation at this

sporting success that had eluded me so cruelly as a table tennis player. All the more so, as it was so unexpected.

Mick Francis revived and was runner-up, finishing 12 and a half minutes after me. All the talk after the race was about the teams for the upcoming 100km 'test event' that was planned to take place just prior to the Commonwealth Games in Victoria, Canada, in September.

This was a big deal for the 100km event at the time, because it was thought that the 100km would become the blue riband of the sport of ultra-running. This never did quite happen and it remains a niche event compared to many other ultra-races.

I was overhearing these conversations and starting to think "I'm the Scottish Champion. I've beaten most of the runners listed as going to Canada, why wouldn't I be going?" There was no simple answer to this. I presume selections had been made and no one had expected a sudden surprise on July 31. I had no understanding of selection criteria, selection meetings and so on.

It was some time before I was able to celebrate my success with Elizabeth, Tanya and Bella. I had to dash from the awards ceremony to catch a bus to Edinburgh Waverley Station ready for the long train journey north with changes in Perth and Inverness and a final stop in Thurso for an overnight stay. Then down to the port of Scrabster for the ferry to Stromness, a bus to Kirkwall and finally the afternoon ferry to Sanday.

I had had many hours to ponder on my shock success. One thing that puzzled me was how I was able to cover the 62.2 miles so comfortably for the first time. My longest runs in training were rarely more than 18 miles. Yet I'd just run 350 per cent further without issue. Yes, my average speed was a little slower and my quads were very sore in the final stages but nothing much else.

That performance kick-started my career in ultra-running and for the next six years 100km races were my main focus. I got my personal best time down to 7 hours 7 minutes 49 seconds – that's 6 minutes 51 seconds a mile, for 62.2 miles.

I went on to complete 18 top class 100km runs and proudly represented both Great Britain and Scotland. I achieved top 20 places in World and European Championships and a Team Bronze in the European 100km Championships in Florence, Italy, in 1997. The following year, I became the World Masters (over 40s division) 100km Champion in Holland.

It was in Italy, just after stepping off the podium in the European 100km Championships, that Elizabeth and I decided to enjoy a week's holiday in Florence. Elizabeth very rarely came to races with me, due to practical difficulties with livestock at home and she, understandably, preferred to go somewhere not dictated by a race venue.

1997 European 100 km Championships in Florence. GB won team bronze medals. I'm first left. Within a fortnight I had been diagnosed with testicular cancer.

Florence, however, was different and her love of opera and all things Italian meant that, on this occasion, she was happy to accompany me.

It was during that week that I started to become aware that my left testicle felt very hard and insensitive. There was no pain, but I felt very uneasy about it. I decided to say nothing to Elizabeth until we got home, not wanting to spoil the holiday. As soon as we were back in Sanday I mentioned it

and in no time at all I was in Kirkwall having an ultrasound scan. The diagnosis was testicular cancer. The treatment was immediate removal.

I was shocked. I felt shattered. I was 43 years old and as fit and healthy as I could be and I had just stepped off the podium at the European Championships. How could this be?

I had hardly heard of testicular cancer and my dad said he'd only come across a single case during his time in practice. Just three months after my experience, testicular cancer hit the headlines when the World Champion, American cyclist, Lance Armstrong, revealed a devastating, Stage 3 diagnosis, that almost killed him.

As I was due to compete for Scotland a few weeks later, in the British 100km Championships in Edinburgh again, I had no option but to make my diagnosis public and withdraw from the event.

Within days I was having surgery in the Aberdeen Royal Infirmary and the good news was that the cancer had been caught at Stage 1, with little chance of spread. However, radiotherapy of the groin area was recommended, plus an eight year follow-up programme. It was agreed I could return later in the year for the radiotherapy treatment.

I had every intention of getting back into my running as soon as possible but I could never have believed how quickly that would be realised. My aim was to try and gain selection for September's World 100km Championships to be held in Holland.

I was home two days after surgery and back at work, bent double to protect my wound, the day after that. I was self-employed, desperate to keep the business going and had a large shed with 500 rabbits needing my attention. Such was my mindset, as a self reliant person, that it never crossed my mind to enquire about any State benefits that might have been available. Years later, I was told that if I had been an employee somewhere, I would have had at least three months off as sick leave!

I resumed walking immediately, covering 40m 'with great difficulty' the next day. I gradually straightened up as my lower body wound healed and the stitches could be removed. I walked every day and by six days I was up to 3.2 miles. I then started doing a run/walk sequence, which worked very well for me.

Six days later and I had managed a five-mile continuous run and announced to Elizabeth that I was returning to full training the next day, July 19, just 16 days after surgery. I gradually increased the volume and intensity of my training from then on.

I had been faxing my training programme to the late John Legge, the British Athletic Federation's Ultra Endurance Team Manager at the time. An intelligent, thoughtful and kind man who, although sympathetic and supportive to my cause, was rightfully highly sceptical of my incredible recovery.

In August, the news came through that I had been selected for the GB Team for Holland! John had fought my corner at the selection meeting and, as often happened, he got his way. This was a huge boost to my battered confidence and I threw myself into my training for the September race.

In brief, I ran the World 100km Championships for Great Britain in Winschoten, Holland, as planned. Tears welled up as I crossed the finishing line in 46th place and seventh in my age category, recording 7 hours, 27 minutes and 56 seconds for the 62.2 miles. A triumph indeed.

Shortly after the race, I travelled down to Milltimber, on the outskirts of Aberdeen, to stay in the Tor-Na-Dee Hospital in preparation for my radiotherapy treatment. This was a harrowing experience, as the majority of the patients were receiving treatment for advanced cancers. I felt very fortunate, but at the same time traumatised by the experience. It was a lifetime low point in my mental health.

In order to salvage my identity and not become a 'cancer patient' , I dressed every day in my GB tracksuit and running gear and went for an easy run every morning, down on the old Deeside railway line, which had been transformed into a cycling and walking trail.

An ambulance would transfer me down to the

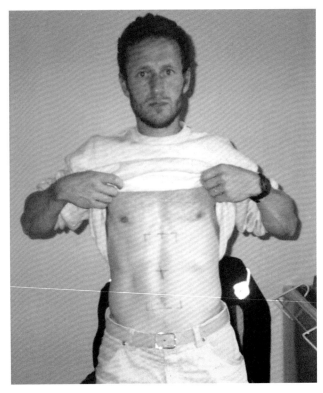

September,1997 and all marked-up ready for my radiotherapy treatment starting the next day. This is the nearest I have ever been to feeling depressed.

treatment area in the main Foresterhill Hospital complex every day. My treatment took only minutes, so I had a lot of free time. After my first treatment I was handed a packet of anti-sickness medication, but I never needed it.

It was impossible to get home at the weekends, due to the travel time involved. The only person I knew of in the locality was a local journalist and runner called Fraser Clyne, but we had never met. He had been an elite marathon runner and he kindly came and collected me at the weekend for a long training run, followed by a meal with his family over in the Bridge of Don. This was very kind of him and made a nice change from the hospital routine.

I attended the thrice-yearly check-ups for three years, then annual ones for a further five years and was then discharged. Tension always arose around the time I reported to the local hospital every year for blood tests, palpation and chest x-rays, but the news was always good. There was no recurrence.

My nutrition rollercoaster

... 'just walk to the finish' ...

Nutrition is obviously important in long distance running; there is any amount of literature and countless "experts" and theories to advise runners; but I learned the hard way and after many unpleasant, debilitating and embarrassing experiences, I ended up going my own way and "listening to what my body was telling me."

This chapter charts my extremely long struggle with stomach problems over many years of competing in ultra-marathons and how they hindered and almost stalled my progress in the sport.

When I started running, I discovered, very early on, that due to a useful and probably genetically enhanced predisposition, I have the ability to derive a high percentage of my energy requirements for running from intramuscular fat metabolism for distances up to the marathon. In addition, by means of a physiological process known as gluconeogenesis, my liver produces and squeezes out just enough glucose into my system to keep my brain happy. I then just need to sip a little water if I feel thirsty.

I became fascinated by the work of the German doctor, Ernst Van Aaken, who advocated fasted long runs and fasting from the evening before a marathon competition, until after the race had finished.

This worked well for me and enabled me to run two marathons in under 2 hours 40 minutes. By the time I ran my best marathon, aged 41, I had experienced three ultra-marathons and had started using dilute carbohydrate drinks to aid my performance. My time of 2 hours 38 minutes 17 seconds in the London Marathon, 1995, was assisted by taking a Leppin carbohydrate gel and a little water, every 5 miles / 8km.

So, for my marathon running career – and other

I've just finished my personal best London Marathon in 1995. The time 2hours 38 minutes 17 seconds.

shorter distances of similar lengths - my nutritional plan was very simple – almost nothing – just run!

As I was so comfortable running on nothing, except a little water, I always did my training runs up to three hours long on nothing, usually just having a coffee, with a little double cream, to set me off. At one point, I wanted to know how long I could last on water only so, during a training run on the Speyside Way, I did a test and got to eight hours of easy running, on water alone. I felt fine, but decided that was long enough.

Nutrition and feeling unwell when running first became an issue for me in May, 1996, when pounding the streets of Moscow. It was my debut in the Great Britain team in the World 100km Championships. It was a big deal for me. I did well, coming home as the second GB finisher and 25th overall with 7 hours 19 minutes and 11 seconds but I had a very sudden one-off episode of projectile vomiting about two thirds of the way through the race. Oddly, no nausea and it had no effect on me at all. It just happened, I felt fine and

I just ran on, but I did ease back on my drinking frequency and volume.

My stomach issues first began to be serious when I stepped up to 24-hour running events, on road and track. Today, with hindsight, these proved to be the *worst possible* races for my stomach.

It's a bit technical but because my chosen running speed of around 6.2 mph /10 kph and above, was right on the point where additional blood would start to be diverted from my GI (gastrointestinal) system to my working muscles, I would start to get absorption problems, stomach contents would back up and vomiting would be the result. Often, I would have very little warning that this was going to happen. On occasion, I would be running well and within seconds, I would be floored by devastating nausea and vomiting. Quite unbelievable.

The first time it really hit me hard was in my 24-hour debut on the 400m running track at Tooting Bec, London, late in 1996. I was the debutant and there were veteran runners in the field, vastly more experienced than me at the longer stuff. I was being watched. The running community wanted to see how I would do. How would I handle the extended duration, the repetitive lapping, the potential boredom? This wouldn't be all over in something over seven hours.

The sudden choking and retching came on hard, sometime after halfway, when I was leading the race and heading for a great debut distance. I suffered overwhelming nausea and sickness. I was bewildered and unknowing.

My brother-in-law, a life-long cyclist, was crewing for me – a thankless task. He saw what condition I was in and advised simply "just walk to the finish". This idea appalled me. I was an international athlete. I was a Scottish Champion, didn't he realise that? However, he was right! My ego had to take its first real beating.

As I had now slowed so much, I was getting cold. It was October in south London on one of those foggy, windless nights. With the vomiting, I was empty and shivering but I started to walk and walk and walk. I saw the sun come up, the temperature dip, then rise again. On and on I went….

I walked until the final gun at exactly 12 noon on October 13. Amazingly, I had won the race, having completed just over 125 miles but it was a very strange feeling. I was claiming victory in my first 24-hour race and yet I felt like a complete failure. Motivation and sheer doggedness had given me victory.

My motivation in the sport was all about *performance* and all roads that would lead me to optimising my performance in competition, whatever that took. I wasn't interested in logging impressive training miles or anything else for that matter, unless it had the chance of producing a better *race outcome*. I was very single minded about that.

The Tooting experience was followed by severe, repeated vomiting in the final hours of the Niort 24-hour road race in western France in November, 1998. I was on the verge of winning this major event when disaster struck and two local athletes passed me in the very late stages, as I could only walk to the finish, being too weak to respond.

After the final gun, I made the fatal mistake of having a quick, hot shower prior to the prize giving, despite feeling exceedingly weak and shaky. Shortly afterwards I was standing on the podium in a crowded but cool sports hall. Suddenly, I felt a very strong desire to go and lie down. I wanted the speeches to stop. I felt cold and very light headed. I passed out, falling backwards off the podium, my fall broken by my right shoulder and luckily not my head.

I came to with a sea of faces looking down at me. I attempted to get up and was told to stay down. I knew what had happened. I knew I was okay, but decided to give in and allow myself the inglorious journey to the local hospital. There, I was warmed up and restored to good health with just a sore shoulder to remind me of what had happened. They kindly took me to the local railway station and I settled down for the long journey back to Paris.

In those days I wasn't so familiar with converting

kilometres to miles and it was only when I worked it all out, while sitting on the train, that I realised the enormity of what I had achieved – almost 150 miles with just the support of a stranger as my helper! Oh my goodness! Despite imploding towards the end and not actually winning, I had run a world class distance, as 150 miles/ 240km is the benchmark for world class running in the 24-hour event.

Two years later in May, 2000, I enjoyed a wonderful win in the Sri Chinmoy 24-hour road race in Basel, Switzerland, at last cruising past the 150 mile mark, recording 153.3 miles/ 246.7 kms at the final gun. I had a sickness issue around the eleventh hour as my race report at the time details:

I've won the Basel 24-hour road race in 2000. I never surpassed my winning distance of 153.3 miles.

"I ran relaxed and well to 11hrs then first vomit (not complete empty out). Well controlled by Buccastem (an anti-emetic pill that controls nausea and vomiting that just sits under the upper lip). Vomiting/nausea seemed to come on after a sustained period of continuous effort. Low patch seemed to spread from 100km – 200km (03 – 0600hrs) during which time I just sipped a soft drink, with then an excellent finish."

The Basel performance demonstrated to me that I was a 'better' runner at longer distances compared to the 100km. It gave me my first ever World Top 10 ranking.

From a race nutrition standpoint, Basel proved to

be a false dawn and I failed to heed the warnings that emerged in Switzerland, being unable to understand fully what I had experienced and what my body was trying to tell me.

This run was followed by a big disappointment in Holland later that year. My Basel win had earned me a place in the Great Britain team for the European 24-hour Road Running Championships being held in Uden in the Netherlands. This was a big deal, as we had a strong team and hoped to do well.

For me, the wheels came off at the eight-hour mark and again at 11½ hours when one of the team managers, Hiliary Walker, suggested some apple strudel to calm my stomach – I immediately threw it up all over her. I didn't quite reach 100 miles in Uden but as a team we did well, winning a bronze medal.

In March 2001, I accepted an invitation to compete in the Soochow University 24-hour Track Race in Taipei, the Taiwan capital. It was my first time in Taiwan and a very different race compared to what I had competed in before. The race was held on a 400m all-weather track and a huge contingent of very enthusiastic students helped to run the event along with a very experienced race director, Frank Kuo. I was determined to have a good performance as I had been invited on the strength of my 153 mile, Basel run the year before.

Although hot and humid by day, the conditions at night were unusual, being humid but cool. This produced rapid cooling and many runners suffered with hypothermia during the night. I was pre-loading with carbohydrate, in powdered form (glucose polymer) prior to the race starting. I had been advised that this was a good plan – it wasn't!

My race report shows what I did:

"Even in the first six hours of the race I had run into severe difficulties:

"Felt full and bloated at start and in early hours. This reduced my intake of race drink from the start and for some hours into the race. At about 6hrs, I got a severe stitch, this reduced my steady

12.4kph pace severely for a little while – it gradually eased. Lower bowel bloating and trapped wind got worse and worse.

"I decided the polymer (either pre-race or in race consumption) was fermenting in the small intestine producing a lot of gas and farting – too much for any comfort whilst running. I switched from glucose polymer drinks to water (a little Coke) and more Dextrose (glucose) tablets.

"Then tried some of the race drink provided by organisers called 'Pokari", a light lemon flavoured glucose polymer drink (8%), electrolytes, vitamins etc) this went down very well until the end with no problems (approx 600mls per hour). No more stomach problems, no vomiting – nice!"

I managed to stabilise myself, stay on track to the end and grab sixth place overall and first in my age group with 188.6 kms / 117.2 miles. But essentially, by my own high standards, my feeding plan had detonated any chance of the top performance expected of me. It had all backfired on me again.

My pursuit of optimal nutrition, experimenting with different diets, vomiting, nausea and stomach problems had now gone on for five years but I was no nearer a solution and any kind of consistency in my 24-hour race performances seemed a far off dream.

During all this time, I had been getting professional guidance.

I was awarded National Lottery funding in 1997 and was able to access sports nutrition advice from experts based at the Scottish Institute of Sport in Edinburgh. I thought this would be a huge advantage in my continuing quest for appropriate nutrition in 24 hour events but it proved to be the exact opposite. What developed was a direct conflict between what the "expert" advised me to eat and what my body wanted.

I was always keen to learn from the science available in sports nutrition journals, seeking the latest information on optimal sports diets. I would then try and apply the suggestions to my own race

plan. This scientific route was very natural to me as I graduated as a scientist from London University in 1976, although I never actually worked as one.

The research papers and my personal nutritionist continually emphasised the need to take in 60g of carbohydrate per hour, which my stomach simply rejected. The route then taken by the sports medics was to treat my symptoms and prescribe various anti-emetics to help stop the vomiting. Sadly, they were treating the symptoms and not the cause. When I reported back to them after races, I was simply not listened to.

I was striving to come to terms with the vomiting, searching for solutions and receiving "expert" advice. I believed in the science and was trying to adhere to what my advisors were preaching. I was always looking for the 'optimal' nutrition plan for me and this led me on a merry dance over a number of years.

I often felt frustrated at myself that I couldn't stop experimenting with my race nutrition. It felt like something I just had to do. But every race was different and it was difficult for me to just repeat a nutrition plan from one race to another.

0-0-0-0

Following the disaster in Brno (see chapter 2) I started to take full responsibility for the nutrition side of my sport. I had allowed myself to become a victim of sports science research. I couldn't let that continue. I had, at long last, come to realise that I had to listen to my body and hear what it was saying. I had to develop the self-reliance, the self-knowledge and the self-confidence to do it my way and that's what I set out to do.

In reality, it was an extremely gradual change in mindset. Deciding to listen to my body didn't happen overnight by any means. It was an alien concept to me and I found it very difficult.

There followed another fruitless experience, this time in Worschach, Austria, in July, 2005, when I was once again overwhelmed by nausea and vomiting after taking in too much in the early stages of the race. I then made the mistake of quitting the

24-hour race early on. It was indeed a sobering experience, once again, walking back along the course towards my accommodation, feeling absolutely "gutted", as hundreds of participants went past, quietly lapping the small town.

It was only some time later that I realised that in these fixed time events there was no need to drop out and quit the race. How you manage your time in the fixed 24-hour period is entirely up to you. I could have had a lie down for as long as needed to settle everything down and then resumed the race. Obviously, I would have lost distance but would have gained self-respect and useful experience instead of going home empty handed once again.

Two years later I did in fact return to this race and had a podium finish, just behind the Greek World Record holder Yiannis Kouros.

Following the disappointment in Austria and as a continuation of my decision to take control of my race nutrition myself, I decided to compete in the Greek classic 153 mile, Spartathlon race just two months later, in September, 2005, and do it in a very simplistic manner.

The Spartathlon is a point-to-point road race which aims to trace the footsteps of Pheidippides, an Athenian messenger sent to Sparta in 490 BC to seek help from the Spartans, against the Persians, in the Battle of Marathon.

The Spartathlon is usually held in late September. Runners have 36 hours to run 152 miles / 245 kilometres, roughly the equivalent of six consecutive marathons, between Athens and Sparta. Runners have to deal with the Greek heat in the day, the cold of the night, and the mountainous terrain. The highest point of the course is Mount Parthenion at 4,000' / 1,200 metres.

There are 75 checkpoints along the way, where runners are disqualified, for safety reasons, if they fail to meet strict, time cut-offs. Many runners have crews that support them during the race, helping them resupply at the checkpoints. However, it wasn't essential to have a crew, as a runner can supply themselves from the checkpoints. Any

non-finishers are picked up by a bus and taken to Sparta.

I decided I wanted to go 'back to basics' this time to try and re-set my nutrition by running on fluids only, as I had done in my now far-distant marathon running career. I would go alone, with no support crew and rely only on the refreshment tables the race provided at 5km intervals. I would carry a 600ml bottle in my hand, using just a wrist strap and have a bum bag containing small packets of pre-weighed Complan meal-replacement powder that I could simply make up as I went along. Complan is a mix of carbohydrate, fat and protein.

I wanted to complete the race comfortably, with no vomiting or digestive upsets and learn the often difficult race route at the same time, with a view to returning at a later date and really racing the event.

I did no nutrition-loading prior to the race or on the race morning. This was a big, major re-set to what I had been doing over the past 11 years.

The result was a huge success and an endorsement of my plan. In short, I ran within myself, using a run/walk strategy and finished strongly in 37th place from 230 starters and 102 finishers in a time of 33 hours 14 mins 20 seconds. I felt elated as I shuffled up the never-ending, tree-lined finishing straight with young kids running beside me. I clambered up the few steps to touch the feet of King Leonidas and claim my laurel wreath.

Another successful finish in the Spartathlon race in Greece.
This time in 9th place in 2007.

"Satisfied" after completing the 2005 Spartathlon in Greece with no stomach issues.

My head was spinning as I was led away to the nearby medical tent for a routine check-up – I was fine and in fact had never felt better after such a long run with no rest breaks. I wasn't just 'fine', I was euphoric!

For the first time, I was able to enjoy the post-race meal and prize-giving and feel like a relatively normal person after a long ultra race. I liked it. But more importantly it was a seismic shift in my own sports nutrition journey. I was in charge of my nutrition plan, which was very unconventional at the time.

However, some elements of my successful Spartathlon plan were misinterpreted and

the subsequent Monaco 24-hour race in November, 2005, was blighted as a result. I was overwhelmed yet again by nausea and vomiting while leading the Apeldoorn 24-hour race in Holland in May, 2006. I was shocked and stunned by this experience (just two months prior to the 135 mile Badwater ultra-

marathon through Death Valley, USA in chapter 8) but the race doctor subsequently gave me excellent advice on hydration and valuable lessons were learned.

By 2006, ten years after I was wiped out in my first 24-hour race in Tooting, I was still plagued by nutritional and vomiting problems. I had taken charge of my diet but I began to appreciate that many other factors were at play, such as weather, race course profile and so on. Nevertheless, I remained positive and optimistic.

I would often start my long trek home from a race feeling deeply disappointed, drained and empty. But after every knockdown, every set-back, I always seemed to be able to glean something positive from the experience and by the time I arrived home there with a glimmer of hope and I would start to feel excited for the next race.

Elizabeth was always completely baffled that I would return to the 24-hour ultra-races, time

Total concentration during a 24-hour race in Switzerland in 2004.

and again, knowing that I might be floored by the nightmare experience of nausea and vomiting. She didn't have a sporting bone in her body and had no interest in athletics, unless I was competing in something. She thought I was putting myself through hell in every race.

Among the failures and disappointments there were successes which fed my belief that if I stuck

I've just won my first race in the USA – a 24-hour event in Phoenix, Arizona.

with it, I would see light at the end of the tunnel. Although my results were up and down, taking personal charge of my nutritional plan stabilised my 24-hour race performances and I started to see some consistency, running distances of between 133 – 138 miles. This latter distance was enough to win the "Across the Years" 24-hour race in Phoenix, Arizona in 2005.

And then there was the Monaco Six Day race in 2006....

The next chapter of this book is devoted to the Monaco race, but it was a game-changer from the nutrition point of view. It was only when I stepped up to multiday racing that I truly achieved my full potential as a runner. My stomach and GI system absolutely loved the slower average speeds and the frequent breaks allowed better digestion. I was laughing all the way to the finish line - literally.

The upsets I had experienced in non-stop 24-hour races simply didn't happen in multiday events and I was able to unleash my full athletic potential in this race format.

Reading through my detailed race reports from between 10 and 20 years ago and with the full benefit of hindsight, I can see that my obsession with what might be 'optimal' was at the root of many downfalls. It seems I couldn't just stick with what had worked in previous races, I was always looking for that little bit extra.

My nutritional obsession with 'more is better' was hard to shift and appreciating that 'I didn't need much' was a lesson that took a long time to sink in.

Feeling the heat! (Picture: Alan Young).

Becoming world class

... 'I felt a surge of energy' ...

I have always answered the question "William, why do you do it?" by explaining that it comes down to my personal curiosity, always wondering what I'm capable of. This applied as much to my 12-year-old self, running to the next village from Sevenoaks in Kent, to me as a 53-year-old heading to Monaco for an event in the world famous marina area that offered entirely new challenges.

I've often said that my real talent was my willingness to try things, because, if I hadn't tried longer distance events, I might have remained a marathon competitor and never realised my full running potential. It was my innate curiosity and my interest in ultra-running in its entirety, that led me to the start line of the "No Finish Line" six-day race in the Principality of Monaco in November, 2006.

My motivation was "just to see what happens". No expectations. No pressure and no pre-event publicity. I treated it very much like my debuts at 100km in Edinburgh in 1994 and my 24-hour debut in Tooting, London in October, 1996. I was dipping my toe in the water and if I didn't like it or just felt that the event didn't suit me, I would drop back down to what I had been doing before.

When quietly trying new events, I would usually choose one that was at the beginning or end of the year so it didn't mess with that year's established race calendar. This was the case with the Monaco race, as it kicked off in early November. As always, I had meticulously researched both this event and the intricacies of running for six days as well, but essentially this really was a step into the unknown.

The "No Finish Line" race is like no other for a variety of reasons. First and foremost, it is much more than just the six-day or eight-day races which are buried within the high profile, mass participation event. This fundraising extravaganza features very highly

in the social and athletic calender of Monaco. The charity that benefits from the whole event is called "Children & Future" and when I was involved in the event it had the patronage of Princess Stephanie of Monaco, who would fire the starting gun.

The mass event is about running or walking as many times as the participants want or can manage over an eight day period. Participants buy a chip and ankle strap from a nearby kiosk and then run or walk one kilometre or a full marathon or as many laps as they want. Many run some laps before work and then return to run or walk some more after work. Every lap is chip timed and recorded. The accumulated distance is then converted into the equivalent number of euros, with one kilometre generating one euro, which is paid by the sponsors to the charity fund. This funding will support projects helping children in the fields of education, health, culture and sport. Mingled within the mass participation event there are the hardcore six and eight-day races.

The spectacular harbour area is the location of the event and a mini-village springs up at race time, consisting of multiple tents and marquees, course markings, timing mats, car and camper van parks, catering and massage tents and so on. This is all going on just a stone's throw from the downtown areas of Monaco and overlooked by the Royal Palace. For multi-day runners who usually find themselves on the fringes of the sport, it all feels very grand.

I travelled to Monaco with my regular crewman, Alan Young, flying to Nice and then using the transfer bus into the heart of Monaco. We arrived the night before the race, as it didn't start until 2pm on the Saturday. We spent the first night in a small hotel in France, just a couple of miles from the race. I actually thought we were in Monaco that night. It was my first time in that part of the world and I didn't realise that France and Monaco just merge into each other. It was on the bus the next morning, heading down to the race location, that I spotted a small sign saying "Monaco" which highlighted my error.

We put up our small tent under the arches that surrounded the pier area and rested while watching the hive of activity, as the race was set up ready for the early afternoon start. The lap length was to be 900m for the first day and thence 1,600m thereafter.

Our base for six days under the arches around Monaco's famous harbour area. (Picture: Alan Young).

We recognised that I was the 'new boy' in the world of multi-day running and although well known in the world of 100km and 24-hour races this was the first time I'd dipped my toe into this hardcore world. We recognised one or two athletes but most were unknown to us. I had a very detailed plan, which attempted to pull together all that I had learned about myself in the previous 12 years of ultra-racing.

IN-RACE Plan

Think **"Fluid - Energy- Sodium – Stomach Lining/Buffering - Alertness"** *Overall target is to 'achieve the greatest distance possible over the 6 days'*

Fluid Plan: *Up to 25deg: Try for approx 600mls/hr (incl Formula volume) Hot (25deg +): Try for approx 750mls/hr (incl Formula volume) Over 30deg: Try for approx 800mls +/hr (incl Formula volume)* **Preferred option**: *Water or 2% drink.*

Energy Plan: *To supply Formula at 6-8% of other fluid volume. Formula - take all-at-once, on the half hour (gives you time to calculate volume based on previous hour's intake of fluid). Two teaspoons of custard on the hour to mop up excess acid, line stomach and provide a little energy.*

Sodium Plan: *Up to 25deg: Aim for approx 0.5g salt (= 200mg Na)/hour in whatever form. Hot (25deg +): Aim for 0.5-1g salt/hour.*

Preferred option: *Depends on temp. Oral Rehydration Solution (ORS) as a salty drink can stimulate thirst and 'clean' sweetness from the mouth.*

- *"Succeed" electrolyte/buffering caps one per hour (= 0.4g salt/cap)*

- *If added, salt in Formula @ 40mls/hr equates to 0.15g salt/hr.*

- *Eat salty snacks.*

Buffering Plan: *To control small intestine inflammation at the start of the race and acid reflux later on.*

- **Preferred options**: *One TUMS antacid tablet/hr OR custard hourly starting at hour 1 (see above). Alternatively liquid Gaviscon (5mls/hr) or*

- *"Succeed" electrolyte/buffering caps one per hour (= sodium bicarbonate and sodium phosphate).*

Alertness Plan:

- *Caffeine intake should, at the very minimum, equate to normal daily intake of caffeine.*

- *Race intake begins at possibly 5th or 6th day as run/walk must extend to achieve distance targets.*

Pace Plan: Run 25mins and race walk for 5mins, from the start. Feeding/walk intervals based on time, which then allows for all eventualities.

On the ½hr: *Formula - 6-8% of other fluid volume (start with 25mls), water or 2%. 1 x TUMS tab if no solid food being taken.*

On the hour: *Custard (2 T-spoons) water or 2%.*

4 hourly intervals: *Eat some cooked food.*

––––

Reading this now, 15 years later, it still looks like a very good plan. Before the race started, we had a visit from fellow ultra-runner Thomas Wenning, from Germany. He was a friend Alan had made at a previous 24-hour race and was in Monaco for the concurrent eight-day race. He was a lively character, with a large moustache, and knew my history of stomach problems. He looked at me with pity as I said I was in the six-day race.

This was a huge step up in distance and duration for me, but also for Alan too. He had only been crewing for me for two years and was struggling at times to keep up with the many changes I was making to feeding and drinking regimes and then mopping up after me when I was overwhelmed with nausea and vomiting. Often it wasn't much fun for him and I respected his stoicism when things were going pear shaped. Now we were both diving in at the deep end with a six-day race! At times, I knew he was wondering what he had let himself in for.

Day 1

Because I was in Monaco to have a very low-key debut in a new, longer event, I felt no pressure and there was no expectation on me at all. Although I was aware that I would be 'watched', it was in no way intrusive. I just set off and stuck to my plan metronomically, with not a care in the world. We were in our own world and just stayed in our cocoon. Every now and then Alan would wander over to the main tent to check the screen to see what distance I had covered and to see what the other 62 runners were doing. The news was good.

By 2pm on Sunday, the first 24 hours was completed

Looking relaxed in the early stages of the Monaco 6-day race. (Picture: Alan Young).

and I had covered almost 100 miles/161 kms very easily and very comfortably. There had been no stomach issues whatsoever. I was happy and loving it. The weather was favourable, being a mild 18 degree during the day and dropping down to a fresh 12 degrees at night. Although at times the course was very crowded, I knew that it would be quieter during the week and overnight. Anyhow, I was running and walking slowly, trying to move as efficiently as I could to conserve energy.

My philosophy was to "allow the distance to come to me", meaning don't push to achieve distance but just allow it to gently accumulate, hour by hour. This was a deep and meaningful mindset and very different from the mental approaches I had used in the shorter, faster races in which I had been successful. It was easier in this new event because I was 'unknown' as a six-day runner and was performing without expectations of any kind.

My morning, short break and night-time routines were also working really well and my make-shift camp bed was sufficiently comfortable under the arches.

Morning Routine:

a) *Wash face, teeth*

b) *Toilet*

c) *Weigh*

d) *2 x "Oats-So-Simple" + honey/syrup, powdered milk, boiling water – leave to soak for about 10mins.*

Can walk a couple of laps while food is being prepared.

End of 4hr session

e) *Shoes and socks off (socks for wash or drying)*

f) *Tracksuit bottoms on*

g) *Sandals on*

h) *Warm, half zip top on*

i) *Eat, drink*

j) *Short nap*

End of day:

Last session before bed

k) *Shoes, socks and chip band off (socks for wash or drying)*

l) *Tracksuit bottoms on*

m) *Sandals on*

n) *Warm, half zip top on*

o) *100g of protein drink in 300mls milk.*

p) *Towel and shower kit*

q) *Bum bag with everything in (watch, chip & band, etc)*

r) *Bed & sleep*

Day 2

Groundhog Day. I just stuck to what I had done on day one. It was working, so why change it. Lapping steadily now on the longer 1,600m / 1-mile lap, I mused at the beautiful harbour setting with the steep hills rising up all around me.

The harbour was full of spectacular yachts which reminded me that Monaco was a tax haven for the rich. It was Sunday afternoon and the course crowding was worse than the day before as families came and enjoyed a day out on the course. With refreshments and toilet facilities available, they could base themselves at the race all day. In many ways it was good to see and emphasised the social value of such events. At times the crowded course did hamper my flow but I knew as the evening drew on, the numbers would dwindle and we would have the course pretty much to ourselves overnight.

A bird's eye view of the harbour with myself dwarfed in the foreground

I noticed that my run/walk plan tended to become just a slow run as the adrenaline subsided and the accumulated distance started to take its toll. My split distance for the second day was 112km / 69.6 miles giving a 48-hour total of 270km / 167.8 miles, a personal best for me and one I had never surpassed even in specific 48-hour races.

Although this second-day distance was a big drop from the day one total, I knew I was feeling good and was deliberately running very conservatively. This 48-hour total was good and I didn't surpass it for another two years and that was in a specific two-day race in France.

Day 3

My 24-hour distance dropped again to 105 km / 65.2 miles. I'm not sure why that was but it still gave me a useful cumulative distance of 375km / 233 miles at the halfway point and more importantly, Alan and I had really got into a good routine and this was being noticed by other runners and crews. We looked like we knew what we were doing, which was quite reassuring.

Furthermore, I was still moving well and was using competitive targets to spur me on. I found this worked really well for me, keeping me motivated and focused, despite rising levels of pain and fatigue. I was having to take painkillers before my long sleep now as leg pain kicked in as soon as I stopped running. The 'long' sleep break was so important, everything had to be done to make it as comfortable and productive as possible although, in the post-race analysis, it emerged that my daily distance wasn't linked to the duration of my sleep breaks.

I never looked at the leader board, as Alan was keeping an eye on things, and I wasn't racing anybody, just doing my own thing, lost in my own world of focus and thoughts. Late on in this third day, Alan mentioned that the race leader was the Frenchman Claude Hardel. He was running hard and was 91km / 56.5 miles ahead of me. I smiled and thought that I might have spotted him, but I wasn't sure.

Alan was having some social contact with other crew members in the kitchen area as they jockeyed for access to the only microwave. I liked microwaved porridge for breakfast and I remember it was always baked solid on to the bowl, making it almost inedible. After the race, I learned that Alan hadn't worked with a microwave before!

Day 4

Moving into the second half of the race, the weather was still holding up well, making good conditions for endurance running. I came past our crew point yet again and Alan rushed out excitedly and yelled "You're closing on Hardel!!"

I was stunned out of my stupor – how could I be? I'm just quietly lapping and lapping and lapping. Alan checked my data – it turned out that I was speeding up as the race progressed! What on earth was happening to me?

My body and mind seemed to have 'trained into the event' as I expressed it. As the hours and days passed, I had got into a kind of groove and my physiology and mentality had become accustomed to the stresses and strains of the huge distances I was accumulating and adapted to them. Now I was able to increase my effort slightly and chase my own challenging targets, which meant that I was also challenging anyone ahead of me.

Next time I came round I slowed and as Alan handed me a drink he explained that, as I was gradually speeding up and Hardel was slowing dramatically, I was closing the 56-mile gap at an amazing rate. I struggled to comprehend the situation, as I had no sense that I was catching anyone. Nevertheless, I felt a surge of energy as my competitive spirit kicked in. I knew I had a powerful urge to compete but it had so often been stifled by gastrointestinal problems that had blighted so many races. Now things were different and I could move into racing mode.

In full flow around the very well-known Monaco quayside area. (Picture: Alan Young).

A little later the familiar figure of Thomas Wenning appeared beside Alan again. Unfortunately, he had had to abandon the eight-day race. I'll never forget the look of sheer amazement on his mustachioed face as I strode confidently past with my head held high. He was an enthusiastic motivator and he stayed on a while to help Alan, enthused by my performance so far.

Sure enough, in the early hours of the next morning, I came up on to the shoulder of a struggling Hardel and swept past him. He immediately stopped running, as if he had been pole-axed. It was a stark lesson into the workings of the mind in multiday running. He then abandoned the race. Years later, I discovered that he had been intent on breaking the six-day world record, hence the intense pace.

Unbelievably, I had clawed back a 91 km / 56-mile deficit and was now leading the race! I felt almost embarrassed and self-conscious. I was a shy, fairly insecure person at the time and now I was being unexpectedly thrown into the spotlight. I had a strange feeling of vulnerability, as I battled to cope with a rising tide of massive physical discomfort which I knew wouldn't go away anytime soon.

Alan was on the point of being a blubbering wreck, as he too was swept up in the excitement. The effect of days of being on-call and having little sleep was wreaking havoc with his mental welfare, more than I knew at the time. Crew have to learn to pace themselves as well as the runner, otherwise they can simply burn out during the event. Prioritising sleep is the single biggest consideration, as it's not possible to stay in a state of 'always on' for six days. In later races, we realised the importance of having at least two support crew.

I was feeling a deep sense of satisfaction because I was now letting my running do the talking and I was having no digestive problems at all. This came as an enormous relief to me and this was reflected in a big increase in distance by the end of the fourth day as I achieved 133 km / 82.6 miles, my largest total since day one.

Day 5

Although Hardel had now gone, the race continued and now I was the one being pursued, with Peter Kluka, a Slovakian resident in France, being the main protagonist. He was camped, by chance, right next to us and we were aware of constant scrutiny from his camp. This helped to keep me alert as fatigue and pain levels mounted.

I felt almost giddy in this new position of being a multiday race leader and being looked at, which made me feel very unpleasantly self conscious. None the less, I stuck to my plan and routines as much as possible. The idea of chasing competitive targets worked really well for me. I used distances I had previously worked out as challenging and now we started looking at the six-day world ranking list for 2006. I aimed at gradually moving up that list.

This exercise was hampered by the erratic updating of the leader board. Alan would frequently wander over to the tent where the screens were and they still hadn't changed. Sometimes there were no updates for some hours, which was immensely frustrating.

Psychologically, I was struggling to cope with the idea that I had arrived here to just 'see what happens' and now I was leading the race and

Exhaustion setting in during the 6-day race.
(Picture: Alan Young).

working my way up the current world rankings. It challenged my mind and my self-perceptions.

Practical problems also started to annoy me, such as having to wait too long to get drinks and snacks I had requested. Running slowly on a mile-long lap meant that having to wait a couple of laps or more, meant that I wasn't getting the supplies for maybe 30 – 40 minutes. In fairness, of course, I had no idea what was happening behind the scenes. After the race, Alan explained his difficulties in getting access to the microwave, clearing up the mess left by other crews and so on.

A very satisfying 134 km / 83.2 miles was my reward for my efforts in day five, consolidating the big jump in distance achieved on day four. The stage was now set for the race climax.

Day 6

Halfway through the final 24 hours the weather finally broke and we moved swiftly from a feeling of late summer to a chilly autumn in southern Europe. Torrential rain was now the order of the day until the end of the race.

I was able to continue with all my routines successfully. Alan maintained his support for me, but struggled with my additional changes of kit and trying to keep our crew area dry. It was simply too much for one person, in a competitive race situation where 'keep moving' was the mantra.

As dawn came on the last day, the final hours were upon me as the 2pm finish loomed. As my mileage grew I was climbing steadily up the world ranking list and this continued to really motivate me – a real carrot and donkey analogy and such a novel position to be in.

I was now experiencing high levels of fatigue and sleep deprivation I had never previously encountered. I was like an automaton, solely focused on running and walking – just one more lap, just one more lap and repeat. Again, and again…. Food and drink just seemed to disappear inside me. I was clinging on to reality, trying to take in my circumstances in a dream-like state.

With everyone slowing and managing their own varying levels of fatigue, it became clear that I couldn't really be caught at that stage and the only thing in doubt was how big my final distance would be and how high I could climb up the world ranking list.

I was still strong enough mentally and physically to really push for those final few hours, as the realisation that I might actually claim the world number one spot became a looming possibility. I was, in effect, chasing the German runner Wolfgang Schwerk's distance from a race in New York earlier that summer. As the last hour came I knew it would come down to the wire, but I was feeling completely spent and had little more to give.

I walked and shuffled those final few miles before eventually negotiating the finishing chute and crossing the chip recording mat for the final time, which my addled brain struggled to comprehend. Suddenly, it was all over. I walked gingerly back to my crew area and Alan and I just looked at each other. Emotions were running high and we were unable to speak.

I had run another 79.5 miles / 128 km on that final day. I had won the race by over six miles / 12 km from the Slovak, Kluka. My final distance came in after a few minutes – 478.61 miles / 770.247 km race. I had become the 2006 World No.1, by pipping Schwerk by just 0.6 miles / 0.97 km!

Furthermore, I had run further in the second half of the race than the first half. This is called a 'negative split' and can be considered a measure of perfect pacing. I had clearly unearthed some, hitherto, unknown ability. It was a huge fillip and boded well for future mega marathons.

Oh my goodness!

Reality quickly hit home. We had a flight to catch later that evening. No time to rest. No time to soak up the atmosphere and the achievement – that would have to come later.

My trophy was presented by Albert II, Prince of Monaco, himself, no less. I felt small and withered as we posed for photos.

Albert II Prince of Monaco looks fresher than me, but I have just run 478 miles to win my first 6-day race!
(Picture: Alan Young).

Then, back to clearing up the detritus of six days of living at the side of a road on the Monaco pier. It wasn't pretty. It wasn't easy for either of us, but Alan was suffering badly. Exhausted, unshaven, sleep deprived. He had sacrificed everything for me. Now he too had to focus on cramming our bags ready for the bus journey back to Nice airport.

I remember us having to wait an insane amount of time for the bus. We were standing at the bus stop and suddenly I felt numb from the waist down. It was a weird sensation. As if my brain had turned off all sensations from my legs, for the time being anyway.

Our journey home was, unfortunately, eventful. Alan was so tired that he lost his passport onboard the flight back to Luton, resulting in another lengthy delay on arrival. Luckily, my ever-patient sister Jenny was meeting us, as it was long after 2am before we were finally heading to our beds.

Three flights later and I crawled out from the small, cramped Loganair Islander aircraft in my island home, Sanday. Elizabeth wasn't able to meet me, but had left our car at the airfield for me to drive myself home.

I sat in Upper Breckan for a while, on my own, in the complete island silence. I still felt stunned, like I was in a different reality. I felt an amazing and very deep feeling of satisfaction. Relaxation washed over my exhausted legs and body. It felt incredibly good.

As always, I kept careful notes recording how I recovered from this massive increase in racing distance. They record that I took painkillers for the first five days after the race. I noted that my biggest difficulty was recovering from the effects of sleep deprivation which I hadn't experienced before. Busily catching up with orders in my small business, it was very difficult to grab enough hours in bed to assist the catching-up process.

Otherwise, my recovery was very good with no injuries and my muscles generally felt good. The pain I experienced post-race was a sort of deep leg and joint pain, unsurprisingly. I wrote that I 'started to feel normal again by the Friday,' which was a week after the race had finished. There was nothing that occurred in the post-race period that was alarming or medically worrying. In fact, the opposite was true. I felt very well suited to multiday running and I looked forward to exploring this intriguing new world.

Psychologically, the race and the result had very deep-seated positive effects on many aspects of my personality. In short, I started to become a more self-confident person.

I felt, very deep down, that my performance had endorsed me as a world-class athlete and sportsman and had justified my long-held belief that I would overcome my stomach issues eventually. Maybe these feelings absolved many of the negative sensations and unfulfilled ambitions that I had carried with me since my sudden retirement from table tennis 15 years before.

One way that these changes manifested themselves was in my attitude to public speaking. Up to that time, I had always felt too nervous, too self conscious and never felt that I was suitably 'qualified' to speak in public about what I did and all that I had learned.

In November, 2011 I returned to Monaco and became the first person to exceed 1,000 km in the 8-day event. I was awarded a special trophy presented by Prince Albert II of Monaco and his wife, Charlene. (Picture: Alan Young).

Shaking like a leaf, I made my debut as a public speaker to the tiny infant class of the Sanday School a few weeks later. I went on to speak, on a regular basis, in many parts of the UK but especially in my home county of the Orkney Islands, with a peak audience of over 300 at the Kirkwall Grammar School.

Over the next few years, I became a regular in Monaco. It fitted well into the late season and I made some good friends there. My performances peaked in 2011 when I became the first person to surpass 1,000km / 620 miles in their eight-day race. This achievement attracted the attention of the general manager of the Hotel Metropole, Jean-Claude Messant, who wanted to bolster his team, of almost 100 staff, who featured in the Business Team event.

I always felt that I needed to have done 'something more', that I needed additional endorsement before I could do that. Now, I really felt that a load had been lifted, I had something worthwhile to say and considered that I might be worth listening to.

He recruited myself and crew into his team the following year, when I managed to clinch the eight-days runner-up spot and the Hotel Metropole won the team event.

I've enjoyed reading a lot.

The hottest place on earth

… 'can I possibly run in these conditions' …

This road event, run through the world's hottest desert, intrigued me from the moment I first heard about it and saw the most spectacular photographs of Death Valley in California with a thin line of white-clad figures running through it. I enjoyed a tingle of excitement when imagining the journey of preparation that would be required to get me from the Orkney Islands, which has an average summer temperature of about 16°C and a highest recorded temperature of 25°C, to Death Valley, California, where 54°C had been measured.

If I took it on, I would have to learn to cope with running a huge distance in temperatures more than double what I was used to, but with very low humidity. I would have to pull together a mandatory support crew and vehicle. I would have to arrange it so that we all arrived at the right time out in the Californian desert, at the tiny hamlet of Furnace Creek in the Death Valley National Park. I would have to raise finance to cover this once-in-a-lifetime trip. I couldn't afford to fail, that was for sure.

It was going to be as much an exercise in expedition planning and logistics, as physical and mental preparation. My university studies in human biology and exercise physiology were going to be stretched to the limit, but a whole lot more too. I would need to take a deep dive into the demands of exercise in extreme heat and consider what would be required, to give me the best possible chance of completing the race, as fast as I could, while being unbroken at the finish.

Ever since I was a young lad, challenging myself to run up to the next village, I always seem to remember thinking that, if someone had done something I admired, then it's possible "so, why couldn't I do that?"

I know now that this 'can do' attitude is certainly not universal by any means. In fact, it seems that many people's initial reaction to something out of their comfort zone is diametrically opposed to mine. They will say "I could never do that!" My answer would immediately be "why on earth not?"

The underlying reasons for these mindsets is clearly complex and goes deep into issues of self confidence and how we each perceive ourselves and our abilities or, more importantly, our inabilities. Personally, I found it hard to understand that if you are watching another human being, who looks exactly like you, doing something you are not accustomed to doing yourself, then why might you draw the conclusion that you couldn't do that yourself? My thought process was always that I could do it, or at least attempt to do it. I would then enjoy the process of finding out how that person trained themselves to be able to do that thing.

The challenges of running 135 miles through Death Valley in mid-summer were clearly achievable, as more than half the field managed it every year. The actual flat Death Valley section was only the first portion of the course, lasting probably seven or eight hours on a good day. The remainder of the course meandered up and down the surrounding mountainous region around Death Valley itself, finishing with a punishing half-marathon distance, all uphill to the portals of Mount Whitney and the chequered flag. These hill challenges tended to be forgotten as everyone focused, understandably, on the really hot part.

Following extensive reading and research, I convinced myself that, even though I lived and trained in one of the cooler parts of the UK, I would be able to prepare in a way that would enable me to successfully complete this race.

I knew that when it came to ultra-marathons, there

was a long list of races that sold themselves as the hardest, the toughest, the most demanding, the hottest or the coldest and so on.

I had already learned to look more deeply at these bombastic claims and examine factors such as the selection process for entrants or could anyone enter? How many competitors were actually finishing these races? How generous were the cut-off times allowed? What were the recorded temperatures in previous editions of the races and so on.

Some interesting figures emerged. For example, let's consider the fabled Marathon de Sable, staged in Morocco in March each year and touted as the "Toughest Footrace on Earth" with an entry fee of £2,800. Competitors must complete six daily stages of approximately marathon distance, in a desert environment with temperatures experienced up to 40°C. Around 1,200 entrants are accepted each year.

On examination, it turned out that there were no performance criteria required and 93.5 per cent of the starters manage to finish, within the time limits, with the oldest finisher to date being aged 80. The reason that the finishing rate is so high is because the cut-off times are very generous. So generous, in fact, that you can walk each stage and still finish in the time allowed. Yes, that does obviously mean you have less time to recover, ready for doing it all again the next day but at such a low intensity, less recovery is required.

There's no doubt the Marathon de Sable is a hot, arduous and very tiring event but the "Toughest Footrace on Earth". Really? Surely, not many finishers would be expected if it was so tough?

When I examined the entry criteria for the Death Valley race – official title Badwater Ultra-Marathon - in 2006, it was a very different story. In the first place, I discovered that fewer than 100 runners would be accepted for this 135-mile, point-to-point, non-stop race with temperatures peaking at over 50° C. It was, indisputably, the world's hottest race. Of that, there was no doubt.

Prospective entrants had to achieve a set of selection criteria, including proof that they had officially completed three races of at least 100 miles each. They then go through an application process, prior to being accepted as an entrant. It was, in effect, an invitation race.

The finishing rates for the previous three years had been 63, 79 and 82 per cent, with the oldest finisher under the 48 hour cut-off being 70 years old. I thought this is getting closer to 'tough' but still do-able!

Since 2015, the Badwater race has been forced to make significant changes to its format, as a result of health and safety regulations issued by the National Parks Service. Those regulations banned daytime running in Death Valley, which, sitting below sea level, regularly exceeds temperatures of 38°C in the summer and recently experienced a 100-year high of 54.4°C.

The evening start certainly resulted in more favourable running conditions but also, possibly, a somewhat diminished challenge. Rather than starting in the high 40°C's, the runners now head out under a full moon, with temperatures in the low 20°Cs. As a result, finishing times from 2015 onward were noticeably faster, with new male and female course records set in 2019.

The entry procedure for Badwater had to begin many months before the race, if I was to have any chance of being invited. I knew that I would receive notification at least four months prior to the race, leaving plenty of time to complete a course of 'heat training' and organise the logistics for myself and my crew.

News came through in late March that I had been accepted into the race. Now the serious planning could start.

Clearly, my heat training had to be absolutely 'top notch' if I was to complete this challenge. Luckily, I had been interested in this subject for many years. In fact, I had first looked into it in the summer of 1980, when preparing to make a summer trip to Beijing to play table tennis in searing heat and humidity. In short, I did a series of sessions during which I completely submerged myself in a very hot bath, while taking my temperature, orally, at frequent intervals. By sustaining my core temperature at a higher than normal level, I was able to pre-acclimatise.

Now, 26 years later, science and experience had moved on, as had the research into the performance benefits of heat training. I made good use of the local library in Kirkwall, which would kindly post me the research papers I requested, Sanday not having a library and the internet being in its infancy. The Badwater race's own website was a mine of information and also had numerous anecdotal accounts of preparing for and running the event.

With heat training in general, there are two methods to choose between, Static, which involves sitting in a sauna and Active, whereby the athlete does their sport in a hot environment, for example running on a treadmill in a very hot room. I decided to adopt the 'Static Method' of heat training using saunas, mainly because it was so well supported by academic research and had been endorsed by many Badwater finishers.

Furthermore, I was able to buy a small, fold-up, infra-red, sauna cubicle to use in my home gym in Sanday and, in addition, I had access to a large, conventional sauna, where the air is heated by a stove, at the Pickaquoy Leisure Centre in Kirkwall. Saunas create dry heat and, of course, that was exactly what I needed to experience prior to arriving in Death Valley.

I drew up a 'Sauna Training' protocol which involved 14 sauna sessions, of which all but two would be in my home, infra-red sauna. I used an 'interval method' of training which involved leaving the sauna when I became too hot – usually after about ten minutes - cooled off for a maximum of five minutes and then re-entered the sauna. Then repeat.

The two sessions I performed at the hotter, Pickaquoy Centre sauna were the first and the last ones and these really proved to me that the process had worked.

On my initial visit to the Kirkwall sauna, I was only able to last for 40 minutes of intervals, before I decided that it was best to stop, as I wasn't cooling down enough in the five minute break. When I returned to Kirkwall for my final session, that duration had leapt to 75 minutes on the top shelf, only leaving for a quick cold shower dowsing, pool immersion and taking a drink every ten minutes. This was hugely heartening for me and gave me a great boost both mentally and physically, creating a belief that I would be able to complete the challenge that lay before me.

In addition to that, I knew that being short (1.63m) and light (58kgs) was an advantage when competing in hot environments. A small person has a relatively high skin surface area in proportion to their body mass, which assists in the efficient dissipation of heat from the body via the evaporation of sweat. Essentially, I have a lot of skin and hence sweat glands relative to my body weight.

Choosing a support crew is as much an art, as a science. The mix of characters and personalities can be supportive or explosive and as the pressure and tension rise, with tiredness, discomfort and stress, cracks can emerge in the most friendly group.

It was mandated by the Badwater race that competitors must have a minimum of two support crew and their own vehicle. There was no limit to the maximum number of crew but vehicles were limited to two. The main issue is that if crew members go down with a heat illness, or anything else for that matter, then the runner's inclusion in the race may be in jeopardy. This happens not infrequently.

Although crewing in ultra-races can often be a labour of love and a thankless task at times, it can also be immensely rewarding, as crew empathise with the athlete and all that they are going through, sharing in their triumphs and disasters. I only had experience of working with a single person crew so this would be a whole new ball game for me too.

In the end, I was grateful to have Scotland's Alan Young from Brechin, a former marathon and ultra-runner, who had started crewing for me two years earlier. Also from the UK would be Tim Rainey, from Manchester, a mid-pack ultra-competitor himself. He had crewed for me before and was also happy to do all the driving, of which there would be a lot. Finally, a Brit based in the USA, Mark Williams, would make up my support crew.

Mark was an accomplished ultra-athlete himself and was, although I didn't know it at the time, the first ever finisher of the notorious "Barkley Marathon," which became infamous following Amazon's film about the race, with the title strap line "The Race that Eats Its Young". Mark was unknown to us personally, but had been recommended and that was good enough for us. On a practical note, being based in the USA also meant that I didn't have to fund his travel, which was welcome news for a stretched budget.

I asked all crew members to undergo some form of heat training themselves and I provided them with details of how to do it. Although they wouldn't be doing much running in the heat and our vehicle would have air conditioning, nevertheless they would be out in the heat for a considerable amount of time. If a crew member became a casualty, that would create serious problems for us and needed to be avoided at all costs.

To go from Sanday to Badwater, Death Valley, California, is an ultra-marathon in itself and took hours of detailed planning and organisation. Flying from Sanday to Kirkwall and then onward to Edinburgh and Heathrow where, following an overnight break, I met up with Alan and Tim for our direct flight to Los Angeles. Because of cost considerations we would arrive just a couple of days before the race, the main acclimatisation having been done prior to departure.

On arrival, we picked up our hire vehicle for the five hour drive to Furnace Creek, located in the Death Valley National Park. I had only ever been to Phoenix, Arizona, so my knowledge of the USA was very limited.

Furnace Creek was one of the recommended places to stay for competitors, as it was just a 20 minute drive from the race start point at the Badwater Basin and had a useful range of facilities, including accommodation, which is why it was our first destination. With Death Valley being 93 per cent wilderness, it was imperative to know where supplies could be bought, both before and during the race.

The wildness of the area really hit us. Shops and businesses of any kind were few and far between, although Furnace Creek Village had a restaurant, café, a general store, and petrol station. The race organisation provided copious information and I had done a lot of homework too. Packing our vehicle with essential supplies was going to be the crew's main job the next day as we counted down the hours to the gun.

I had read the small, self-published volume *Death Valley Ultras: The Complete Crewing Guide*, which proved invaluable to us and highlighted the importance of an ice chest in the vehicle and locating subsequent ice supplies, essential for keeping me cool during the race.

The penultimate day arrived and I wanted to rehearse the following day's short trip to the start line at Badwater Basin – which marks the lowest elevation in North America at 280' / 85m below sea level. I was struck by the incredible colours of the salt flats, the mountains, the rocks, the intense light and the heat of course – it was enchanting and spellbinding at the same time. There is almost nothing at the Basin except a lay-by and a wooden sign confirming the location and the elevation.

The heat was incredible and I had a mental wobble for a few minutes as I asked myself "how can I possibly run in these conditions?" I kept my concerns private and reassured myself, once again, that every year over half the field make it to the finish line, so why couldn't it be me too? I reminded myself that I had done the preparation required and remembered about the spectacular success of my sauna training programme. "I can do this!"

I didn't believe it when I was told you could fry an egg on the tarmac in Badwater. "I was wrong!"
(Picture: Don Charles Lundell).

The race is wrapped in stories and myths, some true and some not so much. It is certainly true that you can fry eggs on the tarmac at Badwater. It leaves a horrible mess, which the Park Rangers hate clearing up. But do your running shoes melt on the road? I'm afraid not! It's a great story but I certainly saw no evidence of it.

For the remainder of that last day, I focused on rest and sleep and allowed my crew to give their full attention to their own duties of preparing the vehicle and stocking it up ready for the upcoming couple of days. The crew needed to work as a unit and the team needed to start pulling together now.

The rooms had air conditioning, which was essential, but I noticed that many people I visited had it set at full power, making the rooms really cold. I didn't think that this was a good idea and in my room I set it just cool enough to allow sleep.

Competitors had been warned not to leave any food in their vehicles overnight, as bears come down to the village and can cause damage, as they try and break in, if they can smell their next meal.

The race is based in the Death Valley National Park, which features a huge range of elevations and diverse wildlife. The main focus of the route is the first 40 miles, the flat section through Death Valley itself, during which temperatures reach their highest. Competitors then travel through places

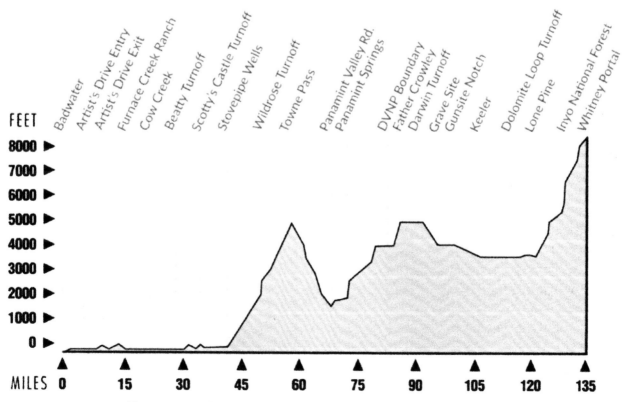

The course profile – not just hot but very hilly too! (Picture: Badwater.com).

with names like Mushroom Rock, Furnace Creek, Salt Creek, Devil's Cornfield, Devil's Golf Course, Stovepipe Wells, Panamint Springs, Keeler, Alabama Hills, and Lone Pine, which is also the race HQ. The course then continues uphill to finish at the Whitney Portal.

The course covers three mountain ranges for a total of 4,450m / 14,600' of cumulative vertical ascent and 1,859m / 6,100' of cumulative descent. Whitney Portal is the trailhead to the Mt. Whitney summit, the highest point in the United States.

In 2006, the race started in three waves, 6 am, 8 am and 10 am. This was to allow runners to be well spaced out on the two-lane highway. The park rangers and race organisers want to keep traffic manageable and well spaced out to avoid accidents. There is tourist traffic as well as all the support vehicles to consider. Being one of the faster athletes, I was allocated the 10am start.

My crewman Mark Williams sprays me with ice cold water while Tim Rainey prepares a drink as I run through Death Valley itself, the flattest and hottest part of the course where the temperature peaked at 54°C. (Picture: Alan Young).

I was dressed head to toe in white, with compression leggings, compression long-sleeved top covered with a loose long-sleeved top, topped off with a cap with neck flap and sunglasses. I certainly looked the part.

We planned that the crew would leapfrog ahead of me and meet me every 10 - 15 minutes approximately. They would pullover on the other side of the road and then two crew would cross over to meet me. They would then hand me my requested drink and or snack, spray the front and back of my upper body with ice-cold water, replace the ice pack under my hat and give me a fresh, ice-filled, neck bandana. I would keep walking at all times as they crewed me, before resuming my run.

When I left them, I would feel wet all over. By the time we met up about a quarter of an hour later I was completely dry again. That was the effect of the heat and the extremely low humidity. It was easy to see why this was the driest place in North America with less than 5cm / 2" of rain per year.

The procedure quickly became routine and the crew rapidly slotted into gear. It wasn't easy for them to trot alongside me, hand supplies over and spray me, watch out for passing traffic and each other, whilst not tripping me up. As I sped off, after one early crew meet-up, I heard a sound, glanced back and saw Tim and Mark tangled on top of each other at the roadside. They had been looking back towards me and had tripped over each other. Easily done, but thankfully only pride had been injured.

About 45 minutes into the race I experienced a sudden awareness "I'm going to be able to survive the heat". I had noticed that I wasn't heating up, the cooling methods and crewing were working and I was running well. My anxiety levels plummeted and I was able to focus on my running and keeping going. The meticulous planning had paid off for both myself and my crew ... so far, so good.

I was drinking on average 840mls/30 fluid ounces per hour during the hottest first seven hours of the race – a huge amount for me, but obviously

Mark Williams runs alongside and sprays me with cold water.
(Picture: Don Charles Lundell).

My energy intake was low, as is normal for me, being just 92 kcals per hour. The temperature, as measured from the car, peaked at 53°C. The intensity of the sun and the overall brightness is hard to describe and the colours were incredible.

The race has only six timing points plus the finish and no aid other than emergency medical assistance is provided, so the crew are kept busy all the time. All the more reason why they must manage themselves well, giving consideration to their own eating and drinking, sleep deprivation and so on. Occasionally, I would ask how the crew were, as I had little idea how they were all coping, being so focused on myself.

required. Over-drinking can be a real danger to health in long distance events, so the crew had a set of scales with them and I was weighed at the start – 61.5kg. After seven hours into the race, I was down to 60.5kg. As long as I was losing a little weight, that was fine.

Essentially, that was the last of the flat running except for the run-in to Lone Pine. With my intense focus on heat issues, I had underestimated the difficulties posed by the very long and demanding hill sections – both up and down. Climbing now

Mark and Tim crew me, foreground right, as I tackle another steep hill. (Picture: Don Charles Lundell).

away from the valley floor and winding my way up to Towne Pass at 1,511m / 4,957 feet – that's almost a mile up from where I started – I suddenly became aware of another severe challenge, as if I needed another one. A ferocious, hot headwind battered me backward and made forward progress very hard.

I hadn't been expecting this and can only liken it to experiencing a car heater, set at its hottest and the blower fan turned full on in your face, during an English summer! My face felt like it was on fire. Everything was drying out and my eyeballs and sinuses felt red and sore.

Step by step and ever onward, I found my way to the top of the Pass and then, immediately faced a prodigious ten mile, steep, winding, downhill run to Panamint Valley. This section put huge pressure on my quads and toes. On the whole, I have always been a good downhill runner and that ability was certainly needed now. It was one of the longest downhill runs I had ever done.

I survived it, except that I knew that my big toe nail on my left foot had been lifted and was badly blistered. With the continual downhill running my foot had moved forward in my shoe, butting up against the front of the shoe and damaging my toe.

I had always been a fanatic about foot care, so I wasn't too pleased about that, but realised that there were no more downhill sections and I would just have to deal with it at the finish, unless it needed attention before then.

I was still moving well across the valley floor but now faced another severe 914m / 3,000 foot climb before a more gentle descent to Keeler and some flat running into Lone Pine. It was now the dead of night and I noticed the incredible blackness of the night sky and the intense natural quietness in this remote region. What's more, as I climbed once more, I noticed I was starting to shiver, I felt cold now! I asked my crew what the temperature was and for additional clothing. "27°C!" they told me. This was both surprising and confusing to my addled mind. "How could I feel cold at 27°C?"

However, as my thoughts cleared a little, it reminded me of how much of our sensations of hot and cold are governed by comparison and contrast, whether our skin is wet or dry and degree of windchill. Consider how you can climb out of an outdoor swimming pool in hot weather but feel cool for a while, especially if there's a light breeze. My body had been 'cooked' for a great many hours and it was now certainly feeling the difference.

I was feeling drained and tired now and my stomach had been queasy. I used TUMS antacid

Being weighed to assess fluid loss and feeling cold when the temperature dropped to 27°C! I was approaching Panamint Pass at 5,300 feet / 1615m. Feelings of being 'hot' or 'cold' are very relative.

tablets to settle my stomach successfully. My fluid intake had much reduced now to between 600 and 700mls per hour and I nibbled on small pieces of banana hourly.

At the Panamint Springs Resort checkpoint at 72 miles, I asked to sit down for a couple of minutes to gather myself. I was feeling 'beaten up' and asked the crew for intensive support for the next five hours to help get me through this bad patch. The crew reassured me that they would be there for me. They knew I was wobbling a bit now.

Although I was pleased with how well I was doing, I was well up the field, I also knew I had to stop thinking too far ahead and what lay before me. I used mantras to keep me focused and to stop my mind wandering.

At 90 miles and 21 hours into the race, I arrived at the penultimate checkpoint at Darwin Turn Off and readied myself for the next leg to Lone Pine, the largest settlement on the whole route. An amazing dawn had been and gone and the day was warming up. At least it was fairly level running now and I was trying to mentally conserve energy as I knew there was a killer climb to come.

At this point I made an unsettling mistake, which took both me and my crew a while to notice. Being relatively flat, we could now see for long distances all around us and I had my eyes glued on a settlement in the distance, which so very slowly got closer and closer. My spirits were gradually rising, as I knew it was 'only' a half marathon to the finish from there. I chatted to the crew about this on a few occasions and they knew it was motivational for me at a difficult point in the race.

Suddenly, they realised that I thought the settlement I was focusing on was Lone Pine – it wasn't – it was the tiny hamlet of Keeler! Lone Pine was another 15 miles further on!!

Oh no! At that stage, the news was a real body blow. My heart sunk and I had to have a mental re-set for a moment and really gather myself to re-focus on Lone Pine.

I had a big boost to my confidence shortly before

My crew vehicle. (Picture: Alan Young).

reaching Keeler when I overtook the controversial American and former Badwater winner, Dean Karnazes. He was sitting in a tub of ice water trying to cool off when I struggled past him into seventh place.

Unbeknownst to me, my crew had been having friendly rivalry banter with the two crews looking after Dean. He had the maximum support allowed by the race, with two large vehicles and a full crew in each. Because of the frequent crewing opportunities and the leapfrogging of the crews and their runner, the crews got to see a lot of each other.

Dean had written a bestselling book about ultra-running that had attracted a new audience to the sport. There was a feeling among the establishment that he wasn't a good enough runner to have become the 'pin up boy' of the sport and to spearhead its growing popularity. He also had a knack for attracting publicity and sponsors, so it's likely that there was hint of jealousy in there too. Once I overtook him, he fell back dramatically.

I finally trudged into Lone Pine after 27½ hours. I was 122 miles into the race, with just 12 and a bit to go. Unfortunately, it was a huge, continuous climb to the finish at the Portals of Mount Whitney at 2,500m / 8,312 feet. That is the point where the road ends and hikers join the trail to the summit of the mountain, which lies at 4,421m / 14,505 feet.

My crew had to really work now to keep me power-walking up this final stretch with an elevation gain of over 1,500m / 5,000 feet in just 12 miles. They were jogging alongside me and shouting and urging me on.

The views were incredible as the road wound round and round the mountain side. There was a heavy rain shower. Temperatures were really dropping now, as I trudged and shuffled up and up. With about 3½ miles / 5½ km to go, I agreed that the crew could leave me, so that they could go on to the finish, get parked up and be ready for me to arrive.

That last stretch, known as the "switchbacks" section of the Whitney Portal Road, really dragged. I was out on my feet. It was one of those situations where you expect to see the finish just round the next bend, then the next one and the next one. I was up on the wooded mountain side now, surrounded by tall pines. A very different environment, compared to that experienced for the previous day and a half.

Eventually, I shuffled round the final bend and there was a short straight and level section with the finishing tape stretched across the narrow road. I picked up my pace and hauled my arms aloft and breasted the tape. I had finished the 'world's hottest foot race' in 31 hours 36 minutes and 12 seconds in seventh place overall and first in my 'over 50' age group. This remains the fastest time by a British male for the hottest, morning start arrangements.

There was no celebration at that point. I just thanked my crew and asked to be driven back to my accommodation as soon as possible. I just wanted to lie down. I was done in!

I was hugely relieved that I had made it and I was pleased with my performance. The intense planning and preparation had paid off, which was very rewarding.

The next morning we drove into Lone Pine and I ordered a huge breakfast of eggs, hash browns and fried onions at a local diner. Unfortunately, my

I've finished! 9th place in 31 hours 36 minutes 12 seconds. This remains as the fastest by a British man to date. (Picture: Badwater.com).

It's a team effort, as always. Mark Williams , Tim Rainey and Alan Young.

eyes were much bigger than my stomach and I just couldn't eat much. I just didn't feel very hungry, which was not unusual for me following long races. The hunger always seems to develop slowly over the following 24 hours.

I mentioned that I was fanatical about my feet and foot care in general. My left big toe had a balloon-shaped blister on the end, so I lined up to have it patched up prior to the prizegiving.

Imagine my surprise when I saw that the gentleman doing the patching was none other than John Vonhof , the esteemed author of a popular book called *Fixing Your Feet*, of which I had several editions.

The morning after. A case of my eyes being very much bigger than my stomach! I should have known better, as my appetite is always very slow to return after an ultra-marathon. I could only make a very small in-road into that lot! (Picture: Alan Young).

Crewman Alan Young supports me at the finish and Tim Rainey takes some pictures.

The world's longest race

... 'I was looking at 3,100 miles' ...

It was just after 10.30pm on a hot and humid August evening in downtown Jamaica, Queens, New York, in 2014. I felt like a zombie, having been running 18 hours a day for 50 days, yes **FIFTY** days. I had stopped being me and become this thing that I was doing. I felt small and light. I was silently howling. Tears were streaming down my face, uncontrollably. I was brushing them away when I passed through the busy pit area. My handler, Alan, must have seen them.

At last, finally, I realised and accepted that I was going to finish this beast of a race. A journey of 3,100 miles was going to end and soon. It had felt like an endless adventure. I never, until now, allowed myself to think that I might finish. Too much had gone wrong and too much might still go wrong, but now it really was coming to an end.

I had done 98 laps today, 53.80 miles run and just seven more laps to go. Could that really be right? It was. My eyes stung with sweat. Despite the late hour, it was still 27°C and the air was heavy with humidity.

My breathing lurched again, as emotions spilled over like never before. Emotion I never knew I had within me. It all came out, it needed to come out, but where it came from I'll never know.

These endless short laps, the heat, the humidity, the crowded pavements, the traffic and endless car horns, the feeling of continuous bone-crunching fatigue and tiredness, coping with pain, the wailing of emergency vehicles flying down the Grand Central Parkway – it would certainly end soon. That I now knew and accepted.

Suddenly, I had a sharp pain in my left knee. Completely out of the blue, unexpected. "Where did that come from?" I didn't want to be in pain during my finish ceremony, so I asked Alan for a painkiller. I had it in my hand, but now I was being filmed for a while. Camera in my face. I didn't want to take the tablet in such circumstances. At last, I could swallow it.

The 0.5488 mile lap was now quiet. The High School was long closed and the play park and games pitches were empty. It was just us, the runners, who now owned this lap, downtown in 'the city that never sleeps'.

Eventually the emotion subsided. There was nothing left to come out. I was finally at peace. I ran and walked comfortably now. Excitement was rising. Anticipation of the wonderful finish, that I had already witnessed for others. It was the greatest and hardest-earned finish in ultra-running. Soon it would be mine.

I was having trouble grasping the idea that something I had not allowed myself to think about for so long, the finish, was now just a few short laps away and I could now expect and allow myself to fully enjoy this glorious moment.

A large crowd had gathered under the pools of light around the race HQ on the wide pavement. Balloons were aloft, a festive archway was ready. Eyes were on me. The impossible was happening. Three weeks in, I had been down and out. "Not a chance" was the murmur. Then came a staggering fightback and now a glorious victory was imminent.

On my penultimate lap, I gathered a large flag in each hand. One, a combined Scotland/Orkney affair, the other, the flag of the sponsors, the Sri Chinmoy Marathon team. I trotted the 105th lap that day, giddy with anticipation. I came round the final bend by the playground and then faced a final long, gentle slope up to the rising din of bells, and cheers and clapping and bright lights.

Suddenly, it was all over. I had breasted the tape

in 50 days, 15 hours, 6 minutes and 4 seconds to cover 3,100 miles. I was the oldest person ever to finish the longest race in the world. A wave of immense relief washed over me. I had accomplished the unimaginable, at the age of 60.

I've completed 3,100 miles! A giant sense of relief and exhilaration washes over me.
(Picture: www.srichinmoyultraphoto.com).

A well-rehearsed victory ceremony swung into action. At first I stood and then a chair was provided. The humid night air meant I was sweating heavily. Dabbing my eyes, my hair plastered to my bronzed, lean face – I wanted to look good for the photos.

Still standing, moments after my finish.
(Picture: www.srichinmoyultraphoto.com)

I held a huge bouquet of flowers, quietly smiling and looking around. Taking in this special moment. My special moment. The Sri Chinmoy choir sang their *Victory* and *Congratulations* songs with familiar gusto.

It's all over and I'm "in a dream of my own making".
(Picture: www.srichinmoyultraphoto.com).

The race director, the wise and eloquent Sahishnu Szczesiul, stepped forward, towering over me. With a smile in his voice, he read out a stunning recap of my race. Statistics, positions, outcomes.

A congratulatory handshake from the race director, Sahishnu Szczesiul. (Picture: www.srichinmoyultraphoto.com).

Familiar faces were beaming at me. A huge cake was produced. I looked like a rabbit caught in the headlights and I felt like one. A huge Orkney flag hung behind me.

I was in an extraordinary dream of my own making.

My crewman Alan Young and I struggle to hold my cake. It's
a long way to run for a cake!
(Picture: www.srichinmoyultraphoto.com).

How did I end up in New York?

For me, the Sri Chinmoy Self Transcendence 3,100
mile race of 2014 was the climax of a 22 year
endurance running career, that had started with
my local Hoy Half-marathon in June, 1992. In fact,
it was my 91st ultra-marathon. However, I was well
aware that, bizarrely, runners had finished it with
very little prior experience and one, a disciple of Sri
Chinmoy, had only ever completed a single 50 mile
race before.

When involved in ultra-running, you become
accustomed to the distances and surfaces that you
currently prefer. You will be vaguely aware of other,
usually longer events, on a range of courses, but
can never envisage yourself doing them and often
you have only mild, or no interest in such events.

Something then happens. A chance comment,
an online feature, a rogue interview on a far-out
podcast and you sense a twinge of interest. Your
curiosity is piqued and you feel the need to find
out more about the event in question. You do and
then you go into a state of denial. Abandoning
such a crazy idea. Then you're hooked!

I think the first time I ever heard mention of super-
long, 'mega-marathons' was in 1996, at my first
24-hour race in Tooting, south London. Another
entrant, Abichal Sherrington, a Sri Chinmoy

disciple, was mentioned to me in connection with
a ten day race in America, but such information
just went in one ear and out the other. I was at the
'no interest' stage.

As my focus gradually shifted towards longer and
longer events, I realised that I would be leaving
behind the chance to represent the national
teams of both Great Britain and Scotland, as
international teams only exist for events up to 24
hours. International representation had been the
cornerstone of my ambitions up to that time.

While I was discussing this issue with my
crewman, Alan Young, one day, he mentioned
that, unbeknown to me, I had already achieved a
number of records at a variety of distances and
intermediate times, both overall and in my age-
group. This piqued my interest and I recognised
that this could be a different way forward for me,
providing a new competitive stimulus and direction,
now that the incentive of international selection
was no longer there.

As my interest in amassing records increased, it was
very obvious that the longer the event, the more
opportunity there was to break existing records and
to set new ones. Clearly, a 3,100-mile / 5,000km
race presented a massive opportunity for me.

By 2012, I was an established multiday runner with
a range of World Age-Group records and overall
British and Scottish records too. The attraction of
the 3,100 was getting ever greater, but how could
I ever arrange my life so that I could do it? How
could I carve out two months from my busy life and
not lose my business and my marriage?

I could see that there were three main hurdles for
me to surmount.

One, was to get Elizabeth's blessing for me to
compete in New York. Going away for a week, for
six-day races was one thing. Pushing that to in
excess of two months was a big ask.

Second, was to get the okay from our major
customers. Essentially, asking them to stock up
for a couple of months, by offering extended credit
if required, was the route to follow for this one.

Thirdly, I would have to get an invitation to compete in the event. There were very few places available with rarely more than 12 runners accepted in total and Sri Chinmoy followers being favoured, as you would expect.

Over the Christmas period, we usually had some time off, as best a self-employed couple can manage; fitting in some local beach walks and catching up on films we had saved for later viewing. Over that week, I deliberately mentioned the 3,100 mile race a lot. Bringing it up in more conversations than I would ever normally have done.

Into the new year and halfway through a lovely walk on the empty, white beach known as Cata Sands, I finally popped the question. "I would like to run the 3,100 in 2014. Would that be okay?" Elizabeth smiled and said that the question hadn't come as a complete surprise. "We should be able to make it work" she said. Phew!

Next, I spoke to our best customer at the time, Katherine, at the thriving K1 Yarns in Edinburgh. "How would you feel if I wasn't around for a period of two months?" "I think we could live with that" came the response. Oh my goodness, two huge hurdles had been cleared.

Finally, I had to continue my conversation with the Sri Chinmoy Marathon Team's race director, Sahishnu Szczesiul. In a race of this magnitude, the organisers are making a huge investment in us, the runners, as well as us, in them.

The $1,500 entry fee, far from covers all the costs, which include a simple apartment for two months in Queens, which must be within a few minutes by car from the course. Full board at the race is required, plus a space in a roadside campervan to rest in during the day.

Essentially, they must look after you for those intensive two months, during which time you will be the most tired and exhausted you have ever been in your whole life. You have no idea how you will react and behave under such duress and neither do they, of course.

While the majority of accepted entrants are disciples of Sri Chinmoy and are running for deeply spiritual reasons, as well as athletic achievement, the organisation welcomes suitable individuals who are outwith the meditation group. I fell into this latter category.

Fortunately, I was very well known to the Marathon Team, having competed in many of their races worldwide, including 100km and 24-hour events. Sahishnu, a scholar of the sport, also knew I had competed successfully in events up to 1,000 miles. Following our email exchange it was agreed, in principle, that I would be invited to the 2014 race.

With that news, the final hurdle had been jumped and barring injury or illness, the way was now open for me to be on the start line in early June, 2014.

With that news, the mental impact hit.

My mind was flooded with questions: "What did I think I was doing?" "Why did I think I could do this as a 60-year-old – it was preposterous!

"I'd never run more than 1,000 miles. Yet, now I was looking at 3,100 miles! Was I mad?"

"How could I possibly complete this challenge?"

To give some context, Land's End to John o' Groats is 874 miles.

And the mental 'noise' continued unabated.

I'd experienced something similar, but not on this scale, every time I had stepped up in distance or duration. It was the 'impossibility' of the challenge that excited me, that drove me on. I had a deep-down confidence in my ability to prepare well, both mentally and physically and to then accept the outcome, whatever that was.

Then I was wondering "could it be done?" And then, "why not?"

I've made a number of references to Sri Chinmoy. So, who was he? He was an Indian spiritual teacher, a Hindu guru, who settled in New York in 1963. Some of his students came to live near him and as a consequence of that, an open Ashram developed around the area where he lived in Jamaica, in the borough of Queens.

Sri Chinmoy was a keen sportsman and he believed that long-distance running, could inspire his disciples to enter a rewarding, meditative state. As a result of this, endurance running became a key aspect of his teachings and he encouraged many of his disciples to start running. Over time, races were then organised, starting with two-milers and climbing to 1,300 miles by 1989.

This growth in Sri Chinmoy events, very much coincided with the 'boom' in marathon running that started in the USA, in the late 1970s and early 1980s and rapidly became worldwide. As a result of this, there was also a concurrent revival of ultra-distance running events organised by national athletic governing bodies in many countries.

Sri Chinmoy then envisioned a 2,700-mile race. The distance was based on his birth date, August 27. It took five years to find a suitable street circuit in the mostly hilly, borough of Queens that might be suitable and permitted by the New York city authorities. Finally, all the necessary permissions were granted and the first Sri Chinmoy 2,700 Mile race was held in 1996 with six participants. A flat, paved course around a park and a school in the neighbourhood of Jamaica, Queens, had been found.

At that time. this was the world's longest certified foot race. At the awards ceremony, Sri Chinmoy announced that the following year, the distance would be increased to 3,100 miles, as a test of physical endurance and spiritual self-transcendence. Sri Chinmoy's birth year was 1931.

Confirmation of my place in the race was confirmed in January, 2014. The die was cast.

My preparation took many forms. Overall, I considered that the previous 22 years of endurance running, 20 of them as an ultra-runner, formed the background of my preparedness. There was immense strength and value in that.

In addition to that, I layered on specific race preparation in the form of heat training, investigating the finer details of the event, the course, the daily routine, the likely weather to be expected, details

of accommodation both at the end of day and during the day and so on and so forth.

As I knew a former competitor, Abichal Sherrington, I decided to fly him from his home in Bristol to Edinburgh, for a two-day interrogation. As I live in Orkney, Edinburgh was a halfway house for us both.

Abichal had lived in New York, as a Sri Chinmoy disciple, for many years and had competed in five editions of the 3,100 race between 2004 and 2008. In those days, competitors could take almost as long as they wanted to complete the distance and Abichal recorded times of between 54 and 58 days. After Sri Chinmoy's death in 2007, a strict time limit of 52 days was imposed.

I came away from this meeting with pages of notes and some valuable insights. I was very grateful for Abichal's input, but it was only when I was running the race myself that some glaring omissions from our discussions came to light.

Abichal had been a New York resident and was completely at home with the crowded streets and noisy, inner-city life. I came from an incredibly remote location in the wilds of the Northern Isles of Scotland. I could step outside my back door and literally see 30 miles in all directions.

Consequently, the noisy, urban street circuit in downtown Jamaica in Queens had a major, unexpected impact on me. It took some time for me to adjust to this alien environment.

Furthermore, Abichal, being a disciple, was an 'insider' and four-time competitor, so was completely at home with the race set-up, the layout, the meal routines and the facilities available in the roadside vans, which formed the pit area. I did not quiz him enough about this and it took me a while to become familiar with the arrangements when I got there, as I was on my own for the first two weeks. As I was to find out, this was not in my favour.

The heat and humidity of summer in New York is legendary. If you can afford to be elsewhere at that time, you arrange to be so. Temperatures of 27-

35°C are considered normal and the humidity can be relentless and draining. Less well known are the torrential downpours, lasting from a few minutes to hours, during which drains back up and become spuming pillars of wetness. I had successfully prepared for the intense, dry heat of Death Valley, California, eight years earlier. Now I would have to endure high humidity as well.

In order to prepare me for this, I lined the walls of my home gym with tin foil, turning it into a heat chamber. Combined with a couple of humidifiers, I could mimic New York conditions while still in Sanday. I did multiple treadmill miles there, coupled with some steam room sessions at the Pickaquoy Centre in Kirkwall. I became accustomed to the uncomfortable and unrelenting stickiness. I comforted myself with the knowledge that at least the temperature would subside after sunset.

0 – 19 days: On the first morning, Sunday, June 15, I arrived at the start area at 5.30am, extra early to give me time to settle in. I was on my own, with no crew support, thinking that would work for the first couple of weeks. I surmised that I was used to running almost 90 miles a day in six-day races and had accomplished well over 70 miles a day in my one and only 1,000-mile race. The required 60 miles per day should be fine.

One of the organisers, Rupanta La Russo, showed me to one of the campervans, parked at the roadside, where I had been allocated a bed for daytime rest breaks. I thought I had a specific bed, but it turned out this wasn't the case. I just had to grab one that was free when I needed it. I was sharing with two other runners, Ukranians, Stutisheel Lebedyev and Savagata Ukrainskyi. Night time would be a room in the house I had been allocated which, conveniently for me, was on 168th Street, right on the course and just 5 minutes walk from the start line. We had a wooden table up against the campervan with plastic crates for our kit. Everything was rudimentary but adequate.

As the 6am start approached, a small crowd of Sri Chinmoy followers gathered to hear Sahishnu Szczesiul, another member of the organising team,

call us forward one by one, introducing us to the crowd with a short CV of our achievements. We took our places on the start line. A short prayer was enunciated and we were off.

Fourteen of us shuffled forward for the first lap of this city block, 5,649 unrelenting laps awaited us, to accumulate the unimaginable total of 3,100 miles. This was the largest field since the event's inception, 17 years earlier. I was the only non-disciple.

There was friendly banter in the early laps. I felt strange and awkward. Out of my comfort zone. Most of the field were toughened competitors, hardened to just this one race, to which they devoted themselves every year. There were no race numbers and fancy lycra here. Just baggy shorts and well-worn T-shirts. I could see that they had rigorous routines for refuelling and resting, burnt into their brains after many years and thousands of miles on this cosmopolitan, city block.

I noticed that many of them moved in an unremarkable way with an almost awkward, minimalist shuffle that was unrelenting. Few of them would have garnered a second glance if they trotted down your local street. There was no glimmer that they possessed the inner power to complete insane distances in an unrelenting race format that is unique in the running world. They were like a highly evolved pack of humans, the ultimate specialists, hunting down 3,100 miles.

I felt very much like an intruder into their private world. How dare I tread this sacred lap? My illustrious CV counted for little among this hallowed company. I felt the sensation of 'imposter syndrome' washing over me.

But in my favour, I was humble and willing to learn. I had a plan, but it was very flexible and just as well. I had devised a timed, run/walk strategy that was well rehearsed to slow me down and to extend my endurance. I had thought the lap was flat, but that turned out not to be the case. After multiple laps, it was clear that there were gradients that would be insignificant to many, but became very apparent to

Pranjal Milovnik, who mentored me in the early days of the race. (Picture: www.srichinmoyultraphoto.com).

us, living on the course for 18 hours a day for two months. It didn't suit my plan.

The thick-browed Slovak, Pranjal Milovnik, a veteran of ten finishes, kindly mentored me. "Walk the uphills and jog the downhills and the flats" he wisely advised. He was right of course and I soon abandoned my timed run/walk plan and did as he suggested. He turned out to be a fascinating character. A business owner from Bratislava, he seemed so slow. How could he have recorded such fast finishing times in the past? I would find out in the ensuing days and weeks.

I'd had little time to explore the dishevelled line of campervans and trailers that formed the race HQ. It took me two days to discover there was a large fridge on one of the trailers. Very handy to store fluids as the warm weather started to get even hotter. Even more frustrating was to discover that I had a small, convenient, fridge compartment, high up above a door in my camper van! Savagata's sister pointed that out after a week of being there.

In the very early hours of the race, I was aghast when I noticed that my right hip was unhappy. I was just getting into my rhythm, when I felt pain and discomfort in the front of my hip. Alarm

bells were ringing in disbelief that this could have happened so early in the race. Luckily, I had a stock of Kinesiology tape with me that, when applied, took the load off the area very effectively. The tape stayed on for the entirety of the race and worked an absolute treat.

The magic number in this race is 109. Although we all want as many as possible, 109 is the average number of laps required every day to accumulate 3,100 miles before the 52-day cut-off. In effect, we all become obsessed with that number, giving us the 60 miles required daily. We felt pleased and well-rewarded when we either crawled or glided past it. If we slipped lower, we knew that the pressure was on and, if it was lower for many days, then the size of the mountain to climb would get ever more impossible to reach.

Although I logged 130 laps on day one, my average over the next three days dropped below the magic 109. To my horror, I was struggling to comfortably pass 109 laps a day.

Despite all my pre-race calculations, I could see that I was missing a helper, a race crew. It was taking too much time to do all the little tasks that slowed me down, broke my focus, distracted me from the job in hand. I was sacrificing eating properly for laps and that couldn't continue. I was grabbing snacks off the race table. The meals provided were just put down on my table in large pots, which I felt were too big to walk around with and yet it felt wrong to just stop and eat when I

The evening sessions were often long, lonely periods.

had laps to do. Also, I was struggling with the vegetarian food. It wasn't to my taste.

After four days, Bipin, one of the organising team, came to me and said I wasn't eating enough. They could see the uneaten pots of food left on my table. I explained my problems. He said they would do anything to help. I requested a bottle of olive oil to help the food slip down better and provide extra energy. I tried to eat something every two hours. That helped a lot.

My first helper, Tim Rainey, wouldn't arrive from Manchester until day 14. It seemed a long way ahead at that moment. He couldn't come soon enough.

My lap average started to improve a little and I was keeping my head above water. But my head wasn't happy. Normally, I slip into 'the Zone' when running but here my mind was unusually active. I was struggling with the urban environment, except very early in the morning and after dark when things tended to quieten down. I couldn't seem to get into the Zone, where I like to reside.

Nobody seems aware that I am running the world's longest race as the heavy traffic heads to Long Island on the Grand Central Highway. (Picture: www.srichinmoyultraphoto.com)

Down one side of the course was the 12 lane, Grand Central Parkway, heading out to Long Island. Almost always busy, the numerous emergency services vehicles produced a deafening shrieking sound that made my head explode. The awful sound seemed much worse than what we have in the UK. The contrast with my incredibly quiet home environment in Sanday couldn't have been starker.

Just getting ready to start Day Seven.
(Picture: www.srichinmoyultraphoto.com).

Showing the strain and the focus needed to complete in excess of 60 miles a day for 50 consecutive days.
(Picture: www.srichinmoyultraphoto.com).

The noise was getting to me. It's the custom in America to hoot when the lights go green to alert the first driver to move off. This intermittent blaring noise from the various traffic-light-controlled junctions we passed repeatedly, was wearing me down. Unusually, it was getting to me.

The race lap was on open city streets, passing the large Thomas Edison High School, one of the toughest in New York, on my home 168th Street and passing a busy Joseph Austin Playground on the opposite 164th Street, with large all-weather pitches on 84th Avenue where the race HQ was located. We were like anonymous, wandering nomads just doing our own thing lap after lap. Some local residents knew what was going on and would acknowledge us, but they were few and far between. In the main, we were completely ignored, even by people we saw at the same time every day. Coming from a close-knit, island community where we largely know each other and always at least give a nod of acquaintance, I found it quite unnerving to be ignored so frequently, by people I felt like I was getting to know.

The crowding could also be a real nuisance to a smooth passage around the lap, especially when the school students came and went each weekday, with a heavy police presence and when the playground and baseball pitches were busy.

Day 14. As the two-week mark approached, I was in a new kind of no-man's land as my previous longest race was the Athens 1,000 Miles in 2010, which I finished in 13 days 20 hours. I really was heading into the unknown.

I was excited as I knew that Tim would arrive that afternoon. I'd been looking forward to being crewed and getting news from the UK. I was hoping my daily distances would start to climb.

Suddenly, my left calf cramps really badly. It feels like something has 'pulled'. I'm immediately reduced to an awkward hobble. My head is in turmoil. What's happening. I've had very few running injuries in my whole career. Why now? All kinds of scenarios were rushing through my head as I was forced to trudge around.

It helped that I had pre-committed to staying at the race for the full 52 days, come what may. There was to be no bolting for home if things got nasty.

In long ultra races it's really important to pre-commit to staying at the race until it ends, as there can be a very strong desire to quit a race when things go wrong for the first time and your primary goals are dashed. This decision can often be regretted a bit later on, by which time it is often too late to resume the race. I had no option but to walk

slowly round, doing my best, but at a loss as to what to do about my situation.

I felt so embarrassed and apologetic as a car pulled up later that afternoon and Tim stepped out, beaming when he saw me. After welcoming him to the race, I broke the news. He had never seen me injured before. That day I limped through 77 laps. A far cry from the 109 needed. I knew I had a crisis on my hands, but what to do about it?

I was very unclear how to go about arranging any kind of treatment. I later discovered that my fellow competitor, Stutisheel from Kiev, could arrange things for me. Massage was provided beside the course for all competitors, usually in the evening, when Mario the masseur, finished work at a local hospital.

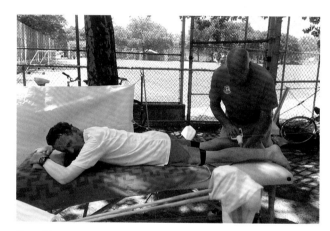

Receiving 'cupping therapy' for my injured calf, which almost cost me the race. (Picture: www.srichinmoyultraphoto.com).

Stutisheel also suggested cupping therapy. I hadn't ever heard of this, let alone experienced it. It was another race volunteer who administered the treatment, which involved placing specially designed, small, clear plastic cups on the injured area and then sucking out the air with a small pump. This forcibly sucked blood and lymph to the area, which immediately went very red. It was slightly uncomfortable, but not painful and left large, raised reddened patches when the cups were removed some time later.

Meanwhile, my mind was in turmoil as I watched the race slipping away from me. It was the first time

When my hips and legs were really aching I found this to be the most comfortable resting position.
(Picture: www.srichinmoyultraphoto.com).

in 91 races that I had sustained an injury during a race. I was also acutely aware that my community 'back home' would be following my progress. Fundraising campaigns were under way and the realisation would be hitting home that all was not going well. As the days went by, my average daily laps slipped lower and lower and I knew full well what that meant.

Fellow competitors and race-organisers looked on with interest. Their looks said it all. I was being written off in the nicest possible way and why wouldn't I be? To come back from such a deficit, as the weather turned seriously hot, was unheard of. It had never been done before, so how could I do it? I had been tested and found wanting. I could simply feel everything melting away from me and I felt powerless. I was in a dark place under my broad-brimmed sun hat. The noisy, inner-city environment, the crowded pavements, the sheer monotony of the repeated laps, broken only by changing direction every day, my disappointing performance – it all came crashing down around me. I felt like I was in meltdown without the tools to cope with it.

I had the cupping therapy, along with a gentle massage, every day and by the end of day 19, I noticed that I could start to move more freely and then managed a slow run without pain. My spirits leapt. Was there still hope? I managed just 84 laps that day.

20 – 46 days: Day 20 dawned warm and humid. I felt like I could cut the air with a knife, as I carefully made my way to the pit area where the two lap counters were getting ready at their tables with lap sheets at the ready for the 6am start. Over the previous six days I had averaged just over 87 laps per day. I was almost 72 miles behind the daily average mileage required to finish within 52 days. Not to put too fine a point on it – I was down and out.

As well as heat and humidity in a New York summer, they also have torrential downpours that can last for either minutes or hours. You have to cope.
(Picture: www.srichinmoyultraphoto.com).

I set off with an easy walk then tested myself, gingerly, by breaking into an early run. I ran and ran and ran. I flowed round the course. I was full of joy with the return of easy movement, my thoughts cleared. It was an amazing feeling. This is what I had come here to do. I crossed the start/finish line just before midnight as the lap counter shouted 115 laps! Oh my goodness, I was back.

Elated, I sat down for a moment and towelled myself down. I then had a moment of great mental clarity and clear focus. In an instant of enlightenment, I suddenly realised that all I had to do was 'to run as far as I could every day' – it's as simple as that. No need to over-complicate anything – keep it simple. I just had to accept, completely, that there was nothing else I could do or expect. Everything else was stripped away to reveal this one simple path.

Obviously, I knew the precariousness of my situation and that one good day doesn't produce a finisher by any means. However, I decided to simply banish such thoughts from my mind and simply focus on doing my best each and every day and then see what happens.

And that's what I did.

I had to resolutely stay in the moment, almost all of every day. If I lapsed and started to consider my position, as others were seeing it, then I was doomed. I had to keep my conscious mind occupied. I had read before that the subconscious mind is the source of one's power to perform and this is what I was now experiencing.

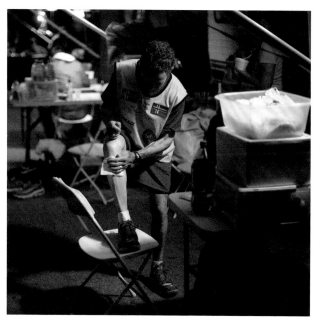

The night time was very humid making my legs feel very sticky. (Picture: www.srichinmoyultraphoto.com).

The night hours often seemed to be long and lonely but it was when I pumped up the mileage.
(Picture: www.srichinmoyultraphoto.com).

In the past, I had used mantras successfully but now, in these circumstances, they had stopped working for me. There were simply too many hours, too many days. I needed something even simpler. I had to stop wishing for what should be happening and embrace completely what was happening – now.

In order to do that, I just focused on my breathing and nothing else. I had to remove any kind of performance expectation completely. I came up with the idea that there was a ball in my lower abdomen and I called it my 'Energy Ball'. I just focused for hour after hour after hour on breathing

into my 'Energy Ball' and that took me to the best place mentally. It proved to me that what we pay attention to when we are fatigued really matters.

I just ran and walked and ran and rested and eat and drank and ran until midnight. I then slept, then repeated and so on and on. Any time my mind drifted, I jerked it back to my 'Energy Ball' and this led me down into deep focus once again.

Somehow, I was able to find solitude within, despite the disordered, inner-city environment that had disrupted my thoughts in those early weeks in Queens.

Many months later I came to understand that I had replaced an outcome goal with a process goal. I had become totally obsessed with the process, the 'doing' and just very occasionally I would peep out and see or hear an outcome indicator in the form of a mileage figure or a prediction.

The deep abdominal breathing led me into the perfect mental state for doing what needed to be done, but it took intense focus and concentration to maintain that state for so many hours every day.

Unbeknownst to me, I developed a reputation among fellow competitors for not talking, for

Humidity was occasionally a little lower early in the morning.

multiple hours, such was my total concentration and focus. Only after the race did fellow competitors hear me speak and laugh and react more normally. I explained to them that to do what I was doing took the most incredible focus and I simply couldn't speak at the same time as being so deeply concentrated. Most of the other competitors listened to music as they ran. That seemed to work for them, but it wasn't my way.

I remember saying to my crew, in a moment of

Day 33 finishes at mid-night. Sitting down felt wonderful after yet another 63-mile day.
(Picture: www.srichinmoyultraphoto.com).

lucidity, that "I have no evidence of how well I am doing". This was, of course, precisely the point and indicated how well I had mentally adjusted to the job in hand. This place of 'not knowing', of being entirely and completely in the now, was one of great peace and inner joy. I was really enjoying it. Loving it, in fact, and my smooth, steady and disciplined running demonstrated this.

A pattern emerged. I would have a slow start, being stiff and tired from the previous day. Then I would get into my stride and notch up 14-16 laps by 8am which seemed to get the day off in the right way. I had then usually passed 40 laps by noon and 70 by 5pm. During the afternoon, I would have taken a one-hour sleep back at my air-conditioned room, during the hottest part of the day.

In full flow with race officials clapping and encouraging me on. (Picture: www.srichinmoyultraphoto.com).

As the evening wore on, the streets cleared, the sun set and then I always, imperceptibly, sped up, feeling that these were my hours. Racing towards the midnight hour, my laps would increase to in excess of nine per hour. It was an amazing feeling – I felt like I was running fast; I felt like I was flying. This happened for night after night after night.

My roommate for 52 days was Ray Krolewicz, a charismatic, 58-year-old, American school teacher from North Carolina. He brought energy, colour and interest to the often boring, long hours on the circuit, when nothing much else was happening.

At first sight, Ray looked an oddity on the course. His hefty figure contrasting with the whippet-like frames of the other runners. Always significant, as the sole US competitor, he was there due to his former friendship with the race's founder, Sri Chinmoy, and his long- standing association with the modern revival of ultra-distance running. He had been an international standard athlete in the 1980s.

My room-mate Ray Krolewicz. He made a lot of phone calls!
(Picture: www.srichinmoyultraphoto.com).

One thing that Ray was very, very good at was talking. As I lapped him, time after time, hour after hour, he was always talking, very loudly, on his phone. I'm not sure how many phones he had, but it had to be more than one. A popular guy, he entertained a string of young female visitors to the course, who would walk a few laps with him, now and then.

Ray only twice made the 6am start, it was just too early for him. He always asked me to give him a shout as I left the room at about 5.40am every day, which I did. A grunt was always his reply. He often used his car to, literally, just drive round the corner

from our room, to the start area. He really was a character.

Ray never left the course early and was always there at midnight, as we all desperately rushed to complete just one more lap. He was also my taxi driver, occasionally giving me a lift back to our room. With the one-way system, we had to go the 'long way' home which took a few minutes longer and I clearly remember how odd it felt to be riding in a car.

Ray was the last competitor to arrive at the race and the first to leave, just an hour after the cut-off time had been reached. This meant that I never really had a chance to speak with him in the way that I wanted. He had an encyclopedic knowledge of modern ultra-running and a wealth of stories about runners and performances from the previous 35 years. Sadly, it just never happened.

When we said our goodbyes, at the race end, Ray very solemnly handed me a white envelope. Surprised, I opened it. It was an invoice for all my taxi rides home. He certainly had a great sense of humour.

At midnight, every day, I walked quietly back to my house, drinking and eating. Replenishing everything that needed to be replenished. I knew the pain would soon come. I experienced little pain while actually running, but shortly after stopping for the day, the pain would hit, usually just after showering and settling down for my four and three-quarter hours in bed. My night always began with a very restless and uncomfortable first hour before finally drifting off.

The days passed and the laps mounted up with encouraging consistency. Although 'only' 109 laps were required each day to just finish, as a competitive athlete I wanted to produce the best performance possible and thus the fastest time I could manage for the 3,100 miles. It was taken for granted that competitors would run at least 100 laps daily and, except for one day, I was in the "mid-teens" (+100) of laps every day. I now felt like a well-oiled machine, churning out the relentless laps.

The relentless humidity was draining and I am pictured
mopping up the sweat.
(Pictures: www.srichinmoyultraphoto.com).

Running through the very busy street of Queens, a vibrant, multi-cultural part of the city, people-watching was a constant source of interest. Even though I saw some members of the public, multiple times, over my 50 days, it was very difficult to make any kind of connection with most people. However, on one occasion, as I trotted along the dusty paving of 168th Street, one hot afternoon, I noticed an elderly 'bag lady' approaching, pushing a square cart with possibly all her worldly goods in it. She glanced up as I approached and in a heavy southern accent yelled at me "get some meat on them thaa bones!". Presumably, commenting on my rather lean appearance. She made me smile and I forgot my tiredness for a few moments.

Sadly, Tim had to prise himself away from the race to return to work, just after I had got back into my running again. He was replaced by Adrian Tarit Stott, the Edinburgh manager of the Run & Become running store. Adrian was a Sri Chinmoy disciple, but was new to the 3,100.

He was intrigued by the event and especially the performances of the highly experienced, regular finishers. He observed that they ate a lot. Snacking nearly all the time. Eating on the trot. Many seemed to take a number of 15-minute rests

with their feet up. They didn't fret over whether they slept or not during the 15 minutes. Pranjal took just one 15-minute rest break a day. Adrian could see that these multiple finishers just kept moving. This explained why some of them appeared very slow, but their finishing times were fast. They hardly stopped moving for 18 hours a day. They were literally human, perpetual motion machines.

I was having regular breaks for fear of breaking down with the relentless lapping. With Adrian's encouragement I started to nibble away at my breaks and stopped having a daily massage, in order to maximise my time on the course. I coped well with this change of plan and it boosted my daily lap count. I also increased my snacking and ate copious amounts of ice cream, which always went down well.

After Adrian's time was up, it was the turn of Alan Young, a regular crewman. He arrived on day 33 and on arrival I asked him how many laps per day I needed in order to finish. He came back with the news that instead of 109 laps a day, I would need an average of 118 a day to have any chance of squeezing under the cut-off time. For a few moments I felt I had been punched in the guts by this news, but, disciplined as ever, I immediately shifted back into deep focus and carried on.

This race gives you a lot, but it also takes away many things. Your whole normal life is stripped away in a revealing way. All of your usual daily

Someone knows I'm in the race!
(Picture: www.srichinmoyultraphoto.com).

routines at home are gone. Your familiar bed, your meals, work and training life and relationships with your family and loved ones are no more. At times you miss things a lot, but mostly you don't as you're so absorbed in the task at hand.

A fellow competitor, Sarah Barnett, was a formidable Australian endurance-running phenomenon, being able to churn out huge mileages in back-to-back multiday races. It wasn't uncommon for her to leave her home in Adelaide and then embark on a series of multiday events in New York, Athens and Hungary in quick succession. Her easy, low stride and flowing dark hair became a feature of the race.

Australian Sarah Barnett, who hugged me during the race and finished just ahead of me.
(Picture: www.srichinmoyultraphoto.com).

It was on one late, humid night, the course was deathly quiet at last and the dim street lights by the school gave a calming aura to the scene. Sarah and I were briefly together, walking a few steps, exchanging a few words and completely alone. She looked at me. I held her gaze and she said "do you want a hug?" She must have sensed something within me, at a very deep level in that instant. Without a word, we hugged each other for a few short moments.

I hadn't touched another human being for many, long weeks. It was both wonderful and cathartic at the same time. A moment of humanity on a warm, sweaty night in downtown New York.

By now of course my performance was getting attention, especially from Sahishnu, a respected statistician and enthusiast for the sport. He came on duty in the late afternoon every day and was in charge until midnight. He had a ringside seat to what was going on.

I was moving up the leader board and my distances were now so consistently in the high teens (+100) of laps a day, that he allowed himself to plot a graph to show where I might possibly cross the 'red line' as it was called, into the 'potential finisher' zone. He apparently kept muttering "this has never happened before, but now it might."

I crossed the line at midnight on day 39 and Sahishnu met me with a huge grin on his face. "You've just crossed the 'red line' with your current total of 2,329 miles."

I had clawed back a huge 72-mile deficit, over the previous 20 days. It had been a phenomenal effort and I felt a rush of elation, which I quickly tempered, as I knew that I still had 770 miles to go!

Alan crewed me with food and drinks from a hand-held basket, every second lap. After 9pm we switched to what we called 'speed crewing' whereby I just had a planned drink every second lap almost without breaking stride, as I flew round those final hours every day. Alan got caught up in the excitement of the occasion and extended and then further extended his stay, to be with me until I finished.

I had to become inured to many sensations

Every picture tells a story!

6am on Day 41. A daily moment of quiet reflection before we start yet another 18-hour day.
(Picture: www.srichinmoyultraphoto.com).

during my weeks on the road in New York. I became completely accustomed to the feeling of being 'always tired'. It was just a feeling that never left me, from rising at 0530 every day until settling back down at about 0100 each night. In reality, I was obviously just recovering enough, all the time, to be able to maintain my seemingly perpetual motion for 18 hours a day.

Sometimes I forgot how tired I was, but small experiences would remind me. I had a small step to mount, every time I entered my accommodation. It couldn't have been more than four inches high. I noticed that, as the weeks went past, I found it increasingly difficult to lift my foot up and on to the step in order to enter my room. While my muscles had become incredibly good at pushing me through over 60 miles a day running, that small change in action was enough to reveal their tiredness.

This well-established race has many traditions associated with it. One of which is that each finisher is presented with a huge cake – it takes two people to move it around and obviously takes some days to prepare. I had so successfully banished any thought of finishing that I was truly shocked and stunned when, with 500 miles to

go, a volunteer, from the race kitchen, asked me what kind of cake I would like when I finished? My immediate thought was "they think I'm going to finish?" I had never allowed myself to think further ahead than the current lap!

The winner, Sarvagata Ukrainskyi from Ukraine, finished in 44 days and 6 hours, followed by fellow Ukrainian Yuri Trostenyuk in 46 days and 14 hours. I managed to maintain my consistent running, notching up lap numbers in the high teens (+100) peaking at 125, 68.6 miles, on day 46. That was my highest total since the first day.

47 – 50 days: Runners were now finishing every day or so and I glimpsed the amazing finishing ceremony that is laid on for each triumphant athlete. We were encouraged to pause a little while and enjoy the speeches, the singing and the emotion-charged interviews. Each time I witnessed a finish, the occasion touched me, very deep down and I allowed myself the luxury of thinking "I want some of that!" We would then slip away and continue our laps while the ceremony continued.

When Pranjal Milovnic finished in 47 days and 13 hours - yet another finishing ceremony - I bent forward to shake his hand and congratulate him as he sat on a low chair. He quickly replied with "soon it will be you." I was stunned that he too thought I might finish.

We were into early August now and the plane trees were changing colour and the potted plants around the race HQ were now past their best. All indicators that I had been lapping there for over seven weeks. Although the summer heat had not been the hottest ever, with many days at 30°C and peaking at 35°C, it was hot enough and the persistent humidity was really challenging, never really dropping much, even at night.

I was now in the most incredible rhythm, churning out over 65 miles a day like clockwork, recovering overnight, then seamlessly doing it all over again. The number of runners was fast dwindling, along with their support crews. The pit area was becoming quieter, the lap counters had fewer

Day 47 and I respectfully sit for a moment to watch the finishing ceremony for the Ukrainian athlete Yuri Trostenyuk, never daring to imagine that soon that might be me too. (Picture: www.srichinmoyultraphoto.com).

well, a late evening finish was on the cards. I was still gripped by my vice of concentration, still not allowing myself to imagine my finish just yet, but that would soon come.

After my finishing ceremony was completed, I stepped on to the course again. I had another 14 laps to go in order to reach the magical 5,000 kms. I had intended to run it, but by then something had snapped within me. The unrelenting vice of concentration had released itself, my drive had eased and I was content to just walk those final laps.

Sahishnu had asked me the day before if I would continue to 5,000 km. He knew I would say 'yes'. Too many records depended on it. I'm very glad I did.

I was in such a rhythm and routine that I awoke as normal at 0530 the next morning and could have continued on as before, but I didn't. Some did. I looked out of my window later on and saw Sarah still lapping the course. She had finished about 11 hours before me.

Goodness knows how many more days I would have lasted. It might have been interesting to find out, but I would have needed an inspiring reason to carry on.

I returned to the course, later on, to enjoy Russian competitor, Jayasalini Abramovskikh's finish. She had been a joyous presence on the course from day one. Seemingly always smiling, incredibly consistent and wonderfully crewed by her mother. She was the last finisher. The race was now over.

I felt a remarkable sensation of accomplishment – a knowledge that I had found a place to which most humans will never venture. That I alone had been to a special corner of the planet, unknown to all others.

Thousands of people have climbed Mount Everest, but I was just the 32nd man, to have conquered the Self Transcendence 3,100-miler.

The statistics speak for themselves. I ran the first half of the race in 27d 01h 21m 21s and the second

runners to focus on and there was a feeling that things were coming to a close.

Day 50 dawned still, humid and hot. I now knew I had just 105 laps, a little over 57 miles to finish, because everyone was telling me and all being half in 23d 16h 17m 42s. To save you doing the maths, I ran the second half 3 days 9 hours 03 minutes 39 seconds quicker than the first half.

I'd like to say that it was due to a masterful display of pacing, but in reality it was produced out of desperation and as a result of a Herculean effort over countless hours and days.

This performance also resulted in a hatful of records at World, British and Scottish level, including age-group records. My overall British records, covering distances from 1,500 miles to 5,000 km are still standing, as of April, 2022.

Given the extreme nature of this event and what it asks of its entrants, it seems quite extraordinary that only one competitor had an injury that required off-site medical opinion.   All other injuries and niggles either cleared up on their own or with help from chiropractors, masseurs, taping, cupping therapy or similar.

My routine after every race was to only start running again when I felt like it. On this occasion I was in good health, injury-free and felt ready after about 12 days.

In the interim, I had spent hours walking Sanday's deserted beaches, immersing myself in my remote location. Loving the peace and quiet.

When I did start running again, on my treadmill, I noticed that my legs were completely devoid of any kind of springiness. They were just dead and my speed had been completely destroyed. I had become a one-pace, slow runner.

It took a concerted, long-term effort, involving repeated, very short interval training sessions on the treadmill, in order to get my speed back.

I didn't race again until seven months after returning from New York.

Sri Chinmoy said: "The fulfillment of life is in the making and manifesting of impossible dreams."

Maybe he was right.

No one had ever run it

... 'I'm losing my hands' ...

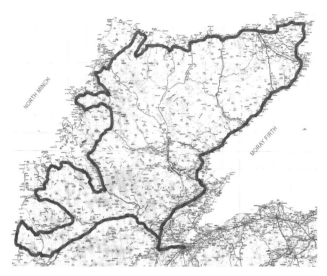

The North Coast 500 route map.

The North Coast 500-mile (NC500), better known as a driving route around the north of Scotland, starts from Inverness, then heads in a westerly direction, before turning north around some of the most remote regions of the western Highlands, across the north edge of mainland Britain and finally down the east coast on the busy A9 back to Inverness.

It is known for quickly changing weather conditions, including extreme winds, for its rugged terrain, featuring the steepest road climb in the UK and for the endless, remote miles of single-track roads with passing places.

Initially, my curiosity in the route had been piqued by reading of a new cycling achievement – a Fastest Known Time (FKT) - having been set for the NC500 by the Scottish long-distance cyclist Mark Beaumont. No one had ever run it before. I thought "why couldn't I have a go?"

The mental challenge was also tempting. Running with no time to beat would be something new for me, having experienced so many events where I was always chasing fixed times and distances and always attempting to break existing records. Here, I would have to just push myself and my crew at all times to simply do the best I could each day. Working with a large crew would also be a new experience, having been used to just one or two helpers at the majority of my challenges.

I was so used to running that kind of distance on loop courses that it took a leap of faith to imagine the logistics involved in tackling an adventure of this nature. Not to mention the possible cold – real Highland cold, compared to just the wind-chill cold I was used to in Orkney.

Highland temperatures were particularly relevant to me because I suffer from an inherited condition called Raynaud's Disease which affects the nervous control of the muscles lining the blood vessels in the extremities. To put it simply, when the temperature drops below about 10°C my hands and feet start to lose their circulation, go very pallid looking and feel cold. The colloquial term 'dead man's fingers' is most apt. I don't have the severest form of the condition, where patients can actually lose digits, but nevertheless I have to take extra care to keep my hands and feet warm.

Running this route would most certainly take me out of my comfort zone in so many ways. Strangely, this was attractive to me and I felt a shiver of excitement at the very thought of it - all those new challenges to overcome.

I would also have to consider which month would be the best to attempt this run. Not just from a weather perspective, but also from the tourism angle. The summer months would have to be avoided so the attempt would have to be in the shoulder months if it was going to happen at all.

I have been writing about an FKT, but what is that? On carefully measured road and track surfaces, best performances can be referred to as records, but on long-distance road, hill and trail routes it's not possible for them to be measured and monitored to the same level of accuracy and the term "Fastest Known Time" has been coined, although colloquially, the word record might still be used. Essentially, an FKT is a self-timed record that modern technology can, to some degree, verify, but it is also up to the honesty and integrity of the runner.

One thing for sure is that if you're going for an FKT, people should know about it. It's not something that should be shrouded in secrecy. It should be publicly declared, well in advance, so that at least enthusiasts can follow the attempt by what's called "dot watching" – observing your satellite tracked 'dot' as you move along the course map. Enthusiasts can then actually come and meet you on the course and see you in action.

Essentially, you and your crew must do everything you possibly can to ensure that you have achieved a genuine, fair performance that can withstand later scrutiny.

Reconnaissance trip

The NC500 interested me, but there was no way I could make a final decision until I had experienced the route myself. To that end, in November, 2018, my crewman, Alan Young, met me off the Aberdeen ferry, drove us to Inverness and the official start and finish point for the NC500, Flora MacDonald's statue, which stands in front of Inverness Castle.

We didn't hang about, but every now and then I hopped out and ran sections of the course. It gave me a feel for the terrain and a different experience of the whole adventure. The route certainly lived up to expectations and the frequency and severity of the climbs and descents in this first half had to be seen to be believed. This route would certainly push me to the limit and in a way that I hadn't been tested before.

Running a short section of the holy grail of British climbs, the Bealach Na Bà, which lies between Lochcarron and Applecross, opened my eyes to the degree of exposure I would experience and the

sapping nature of the unending steep gradients and descents of this winding single-track road. At the same time, the stunning views and the rare sense of true isolation certainly compensated for the brutality of the area.

Quite large sections were driven in darkness on the two days we did it, which meant of course that I didn't get to see some sections of the journey. Our first night was with friends of friends in Ullapool.

We continued onward the next morning passing, through Lochinver and over the bridge to Kylescu, before heading on to Durness with Thurso being our intended destination for that evening. Alan made copious notes and frequent halts as he surveyed the route for potential stopping points for crew vehicles, as well as noting where supplies could be bought along the way.

It was clear that the bulk of the 10,000 metres of elevation gain came on the west side and by the time you get to Kylescu and on to Scourie the hills are behind you. Then there are long, lonely roads ahead where strong head winds are rarely absent. From Durness, one starts to feel that you have returned to civilisation. The road is very close to the coast from now on and after reaching Tongue you feel that Thurso is within reach.

The following day we turned south at last in the direction of Inverness, our final destination. Once past Wick, the traffic starts to build and after Helmsdale we hit the undulating A9

I think we've found one! (Picture: Alan Young).

and I knew that it wouldn't be much fun running down the side of this busy road passing through Golspie, Tain and finally Beauly, before arriving back at the starting point of Inverness Castle.

To end this fact-finding mission, Alan drove me back across Scotland to Aberdeen in time to make the evening ferry back up to Orkney. As I entered the NorthLink ferry terminal he asked "Well, what's the verdict?" I replied "I'm in – I want to go for it!"

Planning for this was of a different order, simply due to the nature of the challenge that faced me. Alan Young was closely involved in the planning, as he had experience of crewing on two Land's End to John o' Groats (LEJOG) runs for other athletes. Alan dealt largely with crew logistics, while I focused on what I needed from the running point of view.

It was decided that we needed two vehicles, a campervan and an estate car. Crew members had to be available in my chosen April window and comprised retired corn merchant Allan Macaulay, experienced marathon and ultra-runner Tim Rainey, retired chemical engineer Ken Walker and Alan Young. Tim would have to leave us sometime through the run but Orkney runner, Erica Clarkson, hoped to join us for the last couple of days, if she could manage the journey from Rum, a remote west coast island where she was working.

Choosing the direction of travel resulted in some debate. In the end, a clockwise direction was decided upon. The direction of prevailing winds was considered most likely to be from west to east and this factor swung the decision for us.

From my point of view, I felt that I would need to increase the amount of specific hill training I would do and also focus on any specialist clothing I might need given the possible degree of long term exposure I might experience. To this end, over the preceding months, I used a hill in Kirkwall as my main training tool. Although living in the relatively flat, northern Isle of Sanday at the time, I usually spent the weekends with my partner, Jessica, in Kirkwall. She lives conveniently close to the long, sharp hill leading down to Inganess Beach, close

to Kirkwall Airport on the outskirts of the town. I spent many a Sunday morning slogging up and down that hill in all weathers.

Given the possibility of days of inclement weather and understanding that I would be on the road for upwards of 18 hours a day I decided that I needed to upgrade my wardrobe somewhat. To this end I reinforced my wet weather gear including the best waterproof socks on the market and multiple changes of other running gear.

Day 1: Saturday, April 13, 2019

I was crouched in the back seat of Alan's car, parked near Inverness Castle at 6:50am on a chilly but dry Saturday morning. The weather forecast, which was eagerly watched throughout, indicated the possibility of a lot of dry weather in the coming days. Could this be true? Had we hit a dry weather spell in this notoriously damp part of the world?

The crew knew that I was not familiar with Inverness and uncertain of my route out of the city, so I might need guidance. The plan was that, at all times possible, I would run on the left, with an accompanying cyclist close behind me for safety.

We are ready for the off. Approaching 7 am on Saturday April 13, 2019 at Inverness Castle and Ken Walker, myself, Tim Rainey and Allan Macaulay stand for a picture beside Flora MacDonald's statue, (Picture: Alan Young).

We had also planned that I would run segments of 3 - 4 hours and then have a short break in the campervan to lie down briefly and refuel.

Aged 65, I felt fit, well prepared and very focused. I departed on the stroke of 7am and trotted over the Ness Bridge and headed out of the city. I was running well and could see the Inverness Crematorium coming up ahead. I had been going for about 40 minutes when suddenly Alan's car pulled up alongside me. Red-faced he yelled through the window "you've missed a turning and you've gone off course by a few miles!" He said it would be okay to be driven back to where I had gone wrong. I queried this and then accepted it and he dropped me back where I thought I had gone wrong.

I later discovered that my eagle-eyed partner, Jessica, back home in Kirkwall, had noticed, from my tracker, that I seemed to be going off course and alerted the crew.

My head was in a spin. This was a serious mistake. Between three and five miles had been added to my journey and time wasted. It should never have happened with all the planning that had taken place. Anyway, it had and I had to draw on all my experience to remain calm, focused and accepting, and to urge myself to stay in the present moment and just focus on my running step by step.

By now I was completely alone and facing on-coming traffic on the narrow road alongside the Beauly Firth. Poor Allan Macaulay, my support cyclist, had been left stranded when Alan Young had rescued me and Allan had to find his own way back on course. We were eventually re-united, after quite some time and normal service was resumed. This whole episode had been quite a shock for the whole team, but everyone was keen to learn from the experience.

Early on, we were surprised at the insane number of Tesco delivery vans that were on the road heading to and fro from Skye, we presumed. They turned off at Strathcarron and the Skye Bridge while we took a right, towards Lochcarron and the Applecross peninsula.

Ken's wife Sue, had provided us with a stock of homemade cakes which were going down a treat. What's more, Sue is a former Scottish Chief Commissioner for Girlguiding Scotland and had kindly put out a request for cakes to Girlguiding Highlands and Islands, who cover that entire region. As a result, we were generously re-stocked at various points along the way.

The rest of the day went well and after a little over 17 hours on the road I had covered 70 miles / 112 kms and we stopped for the night at Kishorn. My watch showed an elevation of just 974m throughout the day, indicating a gently undulating course.

However, we all knew what was coming up the next day – the massive climb up the Bealach na Bà, the steepest ascent of any road in the UK. We were all in the camper van, which proved not to be ideal, but I slept okay.

Day 2: Sunday, April 14

I was back on the road before 6am and heading out towards Applecross. The area really started to feel remote now, with few vehicles in evidence and even fewer people. We felt very much alone.

Mentally, I was steeling myself for the ordeal to come. Although continuing to be dry, it was cold,

Leaving Lochcaron, with Tim for company.

very cold. We all knew that the next few hours would literally be one of the high spots of the whole route, both literally and metaphorically. The Bealach na Bà, the name is Scottish Gaelic for 'Pass of the Cattle', is a single-track mountain pass, with passing places. Built in 1822, it is engineered with very tight hairpin bends that switch back and forth up the hillside with gradients that approach 20 per cent. To the top and down the other side it is 11.4 miles / 18.3 kms and it has long been a huge challenge for cyclists – less so for runners, until now!

The climb started innocuously and I girded my loins ready for the hardest few hours of my life. Mentally, I felt in the right place with steely determination and focused on just breath by breath as always, which brought me right into the present moment. I felt a tingle of excitement.

I had decided to adopt a 3:1 run:walk strategy, whereby I run for three minutes and walk for one. I always run with a small bum bag which contained a 'Gymboss' timing device which 'beeped' to indicate when I would make the switch from run to walk and vice versa. I had used this method in countless ultra-distance races and it worked well for me.

My crew vehicles leapfrogged around me as I climbed. The pass lived up to its name, with frequent sightings of Highland cattle and deer. I was well clad in layers of breathable clothing and a top-level jacket. A headband or hat kept my head warm and I wore thick gloves. Traffic was very light, but still had to make good use of the many passing places, the views were stunning. My support cyclist that morning was Allan, the strongest and most experienced biker on my team. He could look after himself, as well as me.

Before we started, I had alerted my crew that often I might go hours without saying much and that was fine. It was just my way of coping with severe challenges. I'm able to go into an almost dream-like state where I'm completely wrapped up in the activity itself, being only aware of my breathing rhyme.

The endless twists and turns, the crash barriers, the changing scenery. It felt like being on an escalator as I wound my way up and up. After an hour and 18 minutes, I breasted the summit and my watch data indicated that I was now at an elevation of 636 metres. Breathtaking views greeted me as I stopped for a moment, by the spacious car park, to gather myself and looked over towards Skye and the Outer Hebrides. My watch showed a temperature of 7°C, but it felt very much cooler thanks to the stiff breeze.

Looking back down the mountain it was clear to see the incredible, alpine-like, zig-zag road I had just run up. It felt good to have completed this leg of the journey, but I knew the downhill would be tough too. No sooner had I set off to run down towards Applecross, than I noticed that the weather conditions were much colder on this other side, with a biting cross wind, sucking the heat out of me. Running almost continuously down, I wasn't generating as much heat as I had on the way up, which compounded the issue.

I have always been a strong downhill runner for some unknown reason and I certainly needed to be now. Ominously I noticed that my fingers had started to cool which meant that my Raynaud's was kicking in, with the blood vessels in my fingers and hands gradually shutting down.

Soon I had lost all feeling in my fingers and the biting cold was creeping further up my hands, until I had lost all feeling up to my wrists. It was an agonising feeling and I had to take action and quickly. I yelled to Allan that I was 'losing my hands'. Clearly my gloves just weren't up to the job. Allan promptly handed me a pair of top-notch cycling gloves and I grabbed them gratefully, forcing my senseless hands into them with great difficulty.

Mercifully these replacement gloves were better and some feeling gradually started to return to my extremities. This return of circulation is also painful, as tiny blood vessels start to open up again. Feeling very exposed on the mountainside, I was maintaining a good pace and handling the steep descent well. There were a lot of sheer drops on one side initially, but these opened out into a more gentle landscape as I made my way down.

After 52 minutes, I trotted down into the peaceful hamlet of Applecross and saw the wonderful, flat sandy bay there. The place felt quite surreal. It was a balmy 12°C and it felt like a different planet.

Unfortunately, that wasn't the end of my hill running for that day. The Applecross peninsula had more in store for me. The 20km stretch from Fearnmore down to Sheldaig was very challenging running, especially when you consider that I already had the Bealach na Bà in my legs. It consisted of a series of relatively short, steep climbs as I headed inland and then steep descents into small villages hugging the shores of Loch Torridon, Fearnbeg, Arinacrinachd, Kenmore, Ardheslaig and finally, into the quaint village of Sheldaig itself.

About this time we noticed that there were a number of motorhomes and a couple of lassies on bikes that were leapfrogging us every day. We came to recognise each other and got friendly waves from the vans and a few words of encouragement from the cyclists. They were intrigued at how we always seemed to be in front of them. It was of course the 'tortoise and the hare' phenomenon whereby, although I was moving slowly relative to them, I was on the road for very much longer and hence overtook them while they rested and slept. Passing

through Torridon I spoke to one of the motorhome owners and asked if they had any rice pudding – they didn't.

That night I finally crawled into my sleeping bag, somewhere after Kinlochewe, after an 18-hour plus day and just over 62 hard-won miles / 100 kms, covered. My watch indicated I had achieved an elevation of 1,986m / 6,515 feet, that day! No wonder my legs felt tired.

Day 3: Monday April 15

I awoke a bit stiff and tired but feeling 'not too bad', all things considered. In no time I was back on the road with my support cyclist on my tail. Allan, Ken and Tim took turns on the bike while the other Alan focused on leapfrogging ahead of us to give me snacks and drinks as and when required. I was continually snacking, with a more substantial meal awaiting me in the campervan every three to four hours, ideally.

At all times, it was a job for the crew to find suitable places to park the campervan, especially for longer stays in this area of single-track roads.

We were now passing the Beinn Gighe National Nature Reserve and heading towards Gairloch, travelling alongside the beautiful, calm waters of Loch Maree. Soon I was trotting through

Coming off the north end of Applecross heading towards Torridon. (Picture: Alan Young).

Poolewe and then came across the unexpectedly lush Inverewe Gardens. They're in an incredibly sheltered spot and slightly warmed by the Gulf Stream current, which enables unexpected plants to grow there. I could see some of them as I ran past and thought how good it would be to come back and visit another time, but certainly not today.

At the next stop the crew told me that windy weather was forecast. So far, we had been incredibly lucky with the weather, it having been dry since we started. Having set off three days before in waterproof socks, "just in case", they soon came off, as the forecast was proving accurate.

By now I was moving past Little Gruinard Beach heading for Gruinard itself. This was on the edge of the choppy Gruinard Bay, an open area, heavily exposed to the west and described as 'Britain's wildest and least-inhabited corner'. The notorious Gruinard Island was always in sight now. Also known as "anthrax island", it was used for secret British tests with biological weapons in 1942.

It was definitely getting windy now and it was pulling at my Hi-Vis top, emblazoned with sponsors logos! I had been on the road for close to 14 hours and was running with great difficulty down the side of the open sea loch of Little Loch Broom. The crew and support cyclist were getting increasingly concerned about the strength of the wind. It reminded me of very windy runs in Sanday and I kept forging ahead but, at the same time, I made myself aware that this wasn't a solo adventure. It wasn't just about me. The safety of all concerned had to be paramount.

As we approached Ardessie, things came to a head. Allan, my support cyclist at the time, could barely stay upright and we were both being buffeted all over the road by a headwind approaching 50mph / 80kph. We were literally being blown to a standstill. Ken rightly decided that we just had to stop and seek shelter for both ourselves and the vehicles, in particular the high-sided campervan.

This came as a body blow to me. The idea of stopping for any length of time was anathema to

me and just hadn't entered my head until now. This was a time trial, it was a case of head down and run until we got back to Inverness! I took a deep breath, as I put a marker down by the roadside and clambered into the campervan. We headed back to a camp site we had passed, to seek shelter for goodness knows how long. We settled uneasily into the Northern Lights Camping & Caravan Park along with other travellers with the same idea. It was a strange hiatus from the continuous stress and strain of the whole expedition.

It just felt weird and 'wrong' to be lounging around there when I 'should' have been on the road. I had to accept the situation and just breathe and make the most of this unexpected, extended recovery break. It was, after all, a surprise chance to catch up on sleep and nutrition.

Day 4: Tuesday, April 16

The following morning, I was awake early as always and anxious to find out when we could get going again. Too early, as it turned out, as the wind was still wild. However, the forecasts were indicating that it would drop sharply as the morning progressed.

It was just after 9am when I returned to my roadside marker and with Tim behind me, on the bike, I resumed my challenge. Two full run sessions had been missed. A total of eight – nine hours in total. It was a savage blow to my finish time.

It had been quiet, country roads at first, but soon I was on the long and quite busy main A835, heading to Ullapool. As I neared Ullapool, a white van passenger saw fit to empty his collection of empty drinks cans all over me which wasn't great, but was in fact the first act of unkindness on the road I had experienced so far.

Just coming into Ullapool, I arrived to meet my crew at a large lay-by and saw them deep in conversation with a character who had clearly been on the road for a long time. It turned out to be Ian West, an ex-navy guy, who had left Skegness the previous October, to walk around Britain in aid of the charity Guide Dogs for the Blind. Here he was, six months

The only other person I met, on foot, was Ian West, who had been on the road for six months raising funds for the Guide Dogs for the Blind Charity. (Picture: Ken Walker).

later and still walking. We were fascinated by each other's challenges and keen to get 'selfies', before I moved off yet again.

The crew received our first re-supply of Girl Guide cakes in Ullapool. I wasn't involved in the handover and soon I was through the town and arriving at Ardmair, where I passed the 200-mile point. I gazed across to the peaceful-looking Summer Isles before trundling along in the darkness to finish an inevitably shorter, 15-hour day, at Inchnadamph on the southern tip of Loch Assynt. The day had certainly brought more runner-friendly conditions, with the wind easing considerably and just some light drizzle from Ullapool to our stopping point.

After the first night, I had decided to sleep in the

My 'bedroom' for seven nights. (Picture: Alan Young).

back of Alan's estate car on my own, while the crew shared the much larger campervan. This gave me peace and quiet and some time to myself but, with hindsight, I can see that it also parted me from them in some indefinable manner. All being in the camper at the same time had been the only instance when we got together and I got some sense of what the crew was doing and thinking. We lost touch a little as a result of the separation.

Day 5: Wednesday, April 17

It was still dry at 6am and I was soon into my running. I could feel that I was 'training into' this challenge. In other words, I could feel that I was adapting to the rhythm and the specific stresses

Passing Clachtoll Beach near, Lochinver in Sutherland, north west Scotland. (Picture: Alan Young).

and strains of the whole adventure – the rough sleeping, the endless miles, the short breaks and nights, working with my crew and so on. It was a good, weather-beaten feeling and would bode well for the long days ahead.

I was now heading slowly round Loch Assynt, heading in the direction of Loch Inver, although the route turned off just before the village itself and headed on up towards Clachtoll Beach, which was a bedazzling sight as I jogged down towards it. The camp site was quite busy and had facilities which the crew could use. I remembered it well from my recce trip the previous November. Climbing out of the area, I turned a corner and faced a long funeral cortège coming towards me. I stopped and stood respectfully in a field gateway as they passed. I must have looked an odd sight in the bright and breezy sunshine.

Walking across slippery cattle grids was something I had to get very good at. Usually, I was clinging on to something at the same time, to try and stay upright on sore and tired legs.

It's hard to describe the feeling of remoteness out there. This section of the route was like a large semi-circle as I worked my way around the edge of Assynt. I ran on towards Stoer then the spectacular Clashnessie Bay, an expanse of flat, white sand in a memorable setting.

After leaving Drumbeg, I was faced with a series of really sapping climbs in the region of 25 – 30 per

Reaching the NC500 half-way mark on the Kylescu Bridge in north west Sutherland, with Ken Walker keeping an eye on me. (Picture: Alan Young).

cent. These made it difficult to drive up with a car, let alone run or cycle.

It was quite an experience to reach and then run across the spectacular, curved Kylescu Bridge in Lairg, which had replaced the ferry in 1984. It was also another major landmark in my journey as we had reached the halfway mark. We all took a short break in a large car park on the north shore, where we met up again with one of the tourist motorhomes I mentioned on day three. They were intrigued by our exploits and donated towards my charity. We then started the next and final long leg of the day, heading towards Scourie and then Laxford Bridge and beyond.

Running in the pitch black on the lonely roads, somewhere near Laxford Bridge, Allan, my support cyclist and I, nearly jumped out of our skins when a huge black pick-up truck suddenly came up alongside us and then stopped. It turned out to be the head stalker from the Reay Forest Estate, which is located in north west Sutherland. He was out on his rounds shooting foxes. He asked what we were doing and what charity we were supporting. He promptly handed over a generous cash donation and said he'd come back with something for us, which he did. Two large venison steaks, which he handed to Allan! Ken cooked them up a day or so later. A real feast, including a glass of wine, to lift our spirits as tiredness and fatigue had really started to bite in both runner and crew.

Running out towards the remote region around Applecross.

It was another example of a random act of kindness, completely out of the blue and totally unexpected, but much appreciated all the same. It was a lovely end to another 18 hour day and an early hours finish.

Day 6: Thursday, April 18

By now, the morning routine of getting going as soon as possible, without too much faffing, was becoming well drilled. I waited while my support cyclist got himself together and we set off with him a few metres behind me. Often now I noticed that I was awake and ready to go before my crew. I was kind of out-running them. I was comfortable with short sleeps and naps and could run for days like that. However, it was vital that we stayed moulded together as a team. It was a symbiotic relationship, with each of us dependent on the other.

The 14 desolate miles on the A383 from Rhiconich to Durness was wilderness at its best. In effect, I was cutting across the top left corner of Scotland. Durness would be the start of heading across the top of Scotland, as I circumnavigated the Scottish Highlands.

This was a true journey and very different from covering the same distance on a loop circuit. Because I was actually going somewhere, with a destination, I noticed that I got a mental boost at certain points, such as completing a circuit around a peninsula or reaching certain villages and towns.

The picturesque village of Durness is the most north-westerly on the British mainland and the point when I turned a sharp right to begin my journey in an easterly direction for the first time. It was also another Girl Guides cake re-supply point, which always lifted the spirits. I looked down on to spectacular beaches as I jogged through the village and started the long trek inland in order to navigate around Loch Eriboll.

It was on the undulating hills approaching Tongue that I had my first visitor from home. One of my main sponsors, Marty Flett, of the Alfred Flett building company in Orkney. As I approached the support vehicle, from a distance, I noticed there

The only sponsor that actually cycled from Orkney to meet up with me! The indefatigable Marty Flett, cycled 60 miles from the port of Scrabster and found me near Tongue. He did some crewing then cycled back to Scrabster, caught the ferry and was home in time for his tea. (Picture: Alan Young).

were two bikes on the back of the car, instead of the usual one. As I drew closer, it was all smiles as I greeted Marty and Alan regaled him with tales from the journey so far.

He had caught the 6.30am ferry from Stromness in Orkney. A spur of the moment decision he said, when he noticed I was working my way nearer to Orkney. He then cycled the 60 undulating miles to find us, a three-hour ride. I couldn't stop for long, but Marty insisted on crewing me from Alan's car for a bit, which he loved, before he headed back in the Scrabster direction to catch the 7pm ferry back home. I thanked him very much for taking the time and trouble to come out to support me. It was a welcome morale boost. He would be home for his tea later, but it would be four, exhausting days before I would have that pleasure.

Day 7: Friday, April 19

I awoke near the tiny hamlet of Borgie in Sutherland and we were on our way by 0555. With a fair wind and another 18-hour day ahead of us, we hoped to reach John o'Groats some time after midnight, all being well.

The scenery was certainly changing again now, as I ran across the top of Scotland, lipping the coast on many occasions. Incredibly, the weather had so far held for us, having been dry throughout. It was bright and breezy and I put my head down and just carried on doing what I had been doing for seven days now. Left foot, right foot, left foot, right foot and so on and so on ....

The going was 'undulating' yet again with a testing climb about every 10km, or so it seemed. They were nothing compared to what I had already experienced, but nevertheless with 325 road miles in my legs they still made me work.

Before setting off on this FKT attempt, I had seen a mention in the media that Round the World by bike,

'Round the World' cycling world record holder, Mark Beaumont and colleague Si Richardson catch up with me near Strathy, Caithness. (Picture: Ken Walker).

World Record Holder, Scotland's Mark Beaumont would be cycling most of the NC500 on behalf of the Global Cycling Network (GCN) YouTube channel, accompanied by Si Richardson. I sent a friendly Tweet saying I would be on the route and maybe they would pass us at some point and thought nothing more of it.

However, his support crew had bumped into my support crew, back in Durness, so we knew they were coming up behind us. Approaching Strathy, all of a sudden a van appeared beside us with the side door open and someone filming me as I ran along. This was Mark's support team reaching us at last. Next, I heard voices behind me. Mark and Si had arrived.

We exchanged banter and Mark noticed my strange running style, which I explained I had adopted in order to manage running for multiple hours a day during my ultra career. After more videography and a quick selfie they were off. It was quite a fillip and in the resultant YouTube video *Bikepacking Scotland's North Coast 500 In Three Days*, I get a one-minute 15-second slot.

With a spring in my step, I put my head down and ran on. About a mile or so out of sun-drenched Melvich, in Sutherland, I was happily trotting along when I spotted someone dressed to run, standing in an upcoming lay-by and obviously waiting for me. He looked younger than me and very fit. I didn't recognise him, but it turned out to be Rob Turner, the 2018 British 100km champion, who happened to be on holiday in the area with his family, visiting relatives. He wanted to support me by running some miles alongside, which I really appreciated. The roads now were fast and busy, a far cry from what I had been experiencing over the past week.

On reaching the awesome sight of the Dounreay nuclear power station, bathed in spring sunshine, it was time for Rob to leave and I expressed my gratitude to him for making the effort to find me and run about 10km with me. It had lifted my spirits and also relieved the sense of loneliness that can envelop one.

It was cool, bright and very sunny with a stiff sea breeze as I jogged into a rather drab Thurso, in Caithness, a town I was quite familiar with, being so close to Orkney. It was the busiest place I'd seen since setting off from Inverness. I had to 'own the road' as I manoeuvred myself through the main street, over the river and on to the A836 heading towards John o' Groats. The crew decided we should treat ourselves to a fish supper so I placed my order, knowing I wouldn't be able to eat it until later in the day.

Sadly, we had to say 'goodbye' to Tim Rainey in Thurso, as he needed to return to work in Manchester. Partings like this are quite emotional and I could sense how strongly he didn't want to leave the team. His replacement, Erica Clarkson, had got stormbound in Rum and couldn't now join as planned.

Tim also missed out on another cake re-supply, this time from the local Girl Guide group. It was usually a clandestine affair, with an unmarked car pulling in to our lay-by and cakes being handed over and then a quick departure, often under the cover of darkness. This is where the tracker came in so useful, as it made it easy for the campervan to be found. There was one particular cake I took a fancy to, but later noticed I was having to make a lot of sudden dashes into the undergrowth. I asked what it was and Alan replied "Oh, that's date loaf!" That explained it. I had to lay off the date loaf from now on.

The going was pretty flat now and my pace could increase a little as I headed towards Castleton. I was just passing through Dunnet, when an enthusiastic couple rushed out of a camp site, saying they had been following my tracker and suddenly realised I was just passing by at that very moment! They were both keen runners from the Midlands and were on holiday in the area. They ran with me for a while and the cheerful banter broke the monotony for me. They were heading to the Wick Parkrun the next morning.

Near Rattar, I had a short break. I was ready for my fish supper, albeit a cold one. As I crouched

in the back of Alan's estate, he handed me a package. I unwrapped it and could see only the congealed, cold, battered fish. "Where are the chips?" I asked. "You didn't ask for chips!" he replied. I was just about to snap back, but decided to go into Buddhist-mode and say nothing. I just took a deep breath and said "Okay, thanks" We were all deeply tired after seven, unrelenting days and nights on the road. The crew were trying to look after themselves and focus on me at the same time. It was tough for everyone and certainly me, with no cold chips to go with my cold fish!.

Alan chose to stay in his estate car and leapfrog ahead of me with small snacks every 30 minutes or so, while the other three, rotated between campervan driving duties and taking a turn as the support cyclist. It seemed to work quite well, although since Thurso we had been a man down as Tim had departed.

The last few miles from Mey into John o' Groats seemed to take ages, as I twisted and turned and eventually ran down the long straight to the famous place itself. It was in the early hours that I posed for the obligatory photo by the familiar signpost pointing to long distant corners of the world. It was the end of another 18-hour day.

Regarding my own mental state, I was at peace with myself and doing what I did best – staying in the moment and using positive self-talk as and when required. Telling myself how well I was doing, how all I had to do was just 'keep doing what I was doing' and that was enough. Occasional calls home to Jessica also lifted the spirits, as she always sounded cheerful.

I also noticed that as tiredness kicked in, I flickered between feeling overwhelmingly grateful to each crew member, for giving up their time to support me on this venture, to occasional annoyance with them for perceived shortcomings. On one occasion a crew member cycled into me from behind, due to a momentary loss of concentration! Very fortunately I didn't hit the deck as I managed to keep my footing. Another time the crew assured me that a bottle contained plain water, so I dowsed by head to cool off. In fact, it contained a sugary sports drink – my hair was glued to my head and my scalp and face became horribly sticky.

I don't think I ever displayed any annoyance, but that is for the crew to say. We were all over-tired, in our own worlds and locked on to the sharp focus of getting me back to Inverness Castle as soon as possible.

Day 8: Saturday, April 20

I asked the crew to support me in really 'turning the screw' for these last 120 miles. As a result, I was on the road by 0453 and really feeling like I was heading home now. I was moving well, with a good rhythm and enjoying the sense of heading south once again.

As always, eating on the move with Tim Rainey watching over me. (Picture: Alan Young).

In other ultra events, I had been good at doing what I called 'squeezed efforts', whereby I likened it to squeezing a toothpaste tube, so that at the end of the race I had, as far as possible, 'left it all out there'. When I arrived in Inverness I wanted to be totally spent and have a feeling of having 'given my all'.

The roads were still pretty quiet and I could really cover some good distance in these early hours. I was even more 'in the groove', being finely attuned to the rigours of the daily routine. To this end, I noticed that I was speeding up, noticeably and maintaining this increased pace for long hours.

Approaching the bright, sunny town of Wick in Caithness, for the first time, I had pavements to run on, safely separating me from the increased traffic. Reaching the Tesco car park on the outskirts coincided with the 400-mile point – just 116 to go.

We knew there would be a noticeable increase in traffic at Latheron where the A99 joins the A9 bearing traffic from Thurso and the North West. This was indeed the case and both runner and support cyclist had to raise their awareness as we gritted our teeth for many miles on the busy roads. Fortunately, the weather was still being very kind to us with bright sunshine and breezes off the North Sea. Spectacular views, over to the east, were our reward. The next reward was what turned out to be the final delivery of Girl Guide cakes, in the small village of Lybster, 13 miles south of Wick. The cake deliveries, that started in Ullapool many days before, had become a feature of my journey.

I was challenged by an undulating route, with nothing too bad, but I knew the severe hill, known as the Berriedale Braes, was fast approaching. Located halfway between Lybster and Helmsdale, close to the border between Caithness and Sutherland the road drops down steeply, a 13 per cent gradient over 0.8 miles /1.3 km to bridge a river, before rising again at the same steepness, with a number of sharp bends.

First, I had to handle the steep downhill, running fast on the winding, curling highway. At the bottom, my crew were waiting in a car park. I re-fuelled and my legs felt like lead, as I trudged up and out of the depths of the gorge. It was a lengthy slog, but it wasn't too long before my support crew saw me breast the crest of the hill to resume business on the less challenging sections of the A9. It started to get quite cold over the last 20 odd miles to Brora. The crew found a suitable spot to park up for a very short night.

Day 9: Sunday, April 21

I was up and on the road again before 5am. It was Sunday and we all knew this would be the last time for this routine, all being well. Just 69 miles / 111 km to go. I stopped my mind jumping ahead to the finish. I knew I had a challenging day ahead of me and I wanted to stay completely in the present moment, locked in concentration and in the 'now'.

It was a holiday weekend and traffic was heavy. It became bright and sunny and although the air was cool, the piercing sunlight became seriously warm. Golspie and Tain both came and went. The A9 is relatively narrow in places and traffic would often have trouble passing us. It was hot and dusty running down the side of the road, as close to the curb as I could manage. Running in the gutter like this can be treacherous, as all manner of debris gathers there, and yet it's too dangerous to move out to avoid it. My support cyclist behind me decided to ride a few inches out from the kerb to force vehicles to move out a little more than they otherwise might, thereby giving me a little more room in case I stumbled.

Initially, it felt quite dangerous and it probably was but, like everything, you kind of get used to it. The worst thing was when I would hear a squeal of brakes behind me, which was quite often, as an overtaking manoeuvre was hastily abandoned due to oncoming traffic. It was a relief to reach each planned lay-by, for a brief drink and snack and a short break from the pressure of traffic. As I adjusted my clammy clothing, it always felt scary and somewhat dangerous, stepping back into the flow of vehicles to run another stretch.

Not only was I running nearly all the time now, but I was maintaining a faster pace too. Was I smelling the hay in the barn? Approaching the campervan in yet another lay-by, near Evanton, on the Cromarty Firth, I found myself being introduced to the current Scottish Chief Commissioner for Girlguiding Scotland. I must have looked a sorry sight - dirty, sweaty, dusty and clothing plastered to my sticky limbs, as I thanked her for the generous support offered by her members and their families.

I journeyed on through Dingwall and Muir of Ord and on to Beauly. It was late at night now, but most of the roads were well lit, as we were in a more urban environment. I definitely had the feeling that the end was in sight. It was just a case of making sure we had a smooth run-in to Inverness.

Day 10: Monday April 22

It must have been around midnight. We were rounding the Beauly Firth and had about ten miles to go when we decided to just have a final wee break near the tiny hamlet of Kirkhill on the B9164. It was a lonely spot and pitch-black. We were soon up and out again, all 'fired up' for the last leg of the journey.

Allan was my support cyclist as we headed off. I'm not sure how we decided which way to go, but we made our decision anyway. Very fortunately the eagle-eyed Jessica, back in Kirkwall, was having a late night 'dot watching' and noticed, once again, that I seemed to have gone off track. She messaged the crew and it wasn't long before Alan was alongside, telling us to turn round and retrace our steps. We were heading down, directly towards the Beauly Firth and not towards Inverness.

My heart sunk momentarily. This was another shock to the system. At least another 30 minutes had been lost and I felt edgy about getting to Inverness without more navigational errors spoiling the final finishing time. Although I was essentially racing against myself, at heart I'm still a competitive athlete and I wanted the fastest time possible, knowing that at some point, others would come along and attempt to beat my time. I wanted to make it as difficult as possible for them.

From then on, Alan drove a little in front of us, to ensure there would be no more errors. The roads were empty. It was the early hours of Monday morning, for goodness sake, but we wanted a simple run through to the finish.

The final miles were uneventful and soon I was running down the middle of the deserted main road into Inverness and crossing the Ness Bridge once again, ignoring the traffic lights as I went up the final hill, turned right and right again. As I made a last surge towards the feet of Flora MacDonald, Ken called out "Welcome to Edinburgh Castle!". In his own exhaustion he had forgotten where we were – Inverness Castle of course!

I touched down at precisely 02:07:07am on Monday morning, April 21,· 2019. My final day had been 21 hours 23 minutes and 53 seconds.

I appeared tired and gaunt as I leant back against the plinth of Flora MacDonald's statue and Allan conducted a short video interview. I was thoroughly drained, sun browned and exhausted as I mentioned that I hadn't slept for 24 hours. I spoke about the effects of running into headwinds

I've done it! The NC500 has been run for the very first time in 8 days 19 hours 7 minutes and 7 seconds precisely.
(Picture: Alan Young).

for hours on end and about the encouragement along the course from tourists and locals alike.

The NC500 had been run for the first time in 8 days 19 hours 7 minutes and 7 seconds precisely. The time and tracking data provided was subsequently validated by www.fastestknowntime.com.

Part of the 1,000 mile race lap in Athens (Photograph: Alan Young).

A city with two tales

… 'the worst I experienced' …

It was Tuesday, February 4, 2020, and I lay prostrate in Accident & Emergency at my local hospital in Orkney. I was utterly exhausted.

The petite Zimbabwean trainee surgeon, Dr Tariro Gandiya, raised the long, needle-like instrument high above my swollen abdomen and swiftly plunged it down through my abdominal wall just above my pubic bone. A compressed spout of stale urine shot out in all directions, soaking Dr Gandiya, her senior associate and myself. We spontaneously broke into nervous laughter.

It was the end of ten days of unrelenting agony for me. I had spent eight hours under the bright A & E lights but, before that, relentless days of toil with minimal sleep and struggling to cope with acute abdominal pain while "on the road"….

My problems had begun more than 2,000 miles away in far off Greece ….

I was in Athens, where I had entered a 1,000-mile 2020 race. With 109 ultra-endurance races under my belt, I thought I'd have a crack at this much shorter distance, staged in part of a massive former and decaying 2004 Olympic Games complex in Loutraki, south of the Capital

The race had an unusual aspect, inasmuch as 150m of the lap was indoors. This was a very practical difference, as it meant that all the refreshment tables, score boards, crew areas, toilets and showers were undercover and protected from whatever weather Athens in mid-January could throw at us.

The race organiser, was the enigmatic Greek cancer doctor, Costas Baxevanis, who had arranged an almost annual, "International Ultramarathon Festival", since 2005. The 1,000-mile race was just one part of a festival of eight, super-long distance races that Costas was staging.

When my crewman Alan Young and I walked the course, the day before my start, we thought it looked fine enough. The surface was good, no tight corners and a very gentle slope which we didn't consider a problem.

Wrong!

Even after 109 races, it was still easy to make an error of judgment. That 'gentle slope' became a Mount Everest over time and significantly affected my performance.

My accommodation was the now abandoned court, changing rooms, showers and toilets associated with the Olympic basketball tournament. They would have been all first class in 2004 but, 16 years later, they were in need of some tender loving care. It felt like being in a bunker, insulated from light and sound, but it was going to be 'home' for the next two weeks. My crew of Alan Young and Tim Rainey had their own separate area and Orkney's Erica Clarkson was due to arrive for a short spell of crewing at a later date.

My main goal was to break the over-65, age-group record for the distance set in New York in 2004 by the Russian, Vladimir Glazkov. Given a good run, I thought his time of 15 days 2 hours 50 minutes was within my grasp.

As always in these multiday races, the early hours and days are all about setting a routine, a rhythm for both runner and crew. It was strange running both indoors and then outdoors but overall it was of benefit, especially to the support crews.

In reality, I was only undercover for a very short time and 'in touch' with my crew for even less, as I trotted by, grabbing a drink or snack as I passed. Good communication with my support crew was an issue in all my races. Once an event had started there was, in effect, 'no time' to communicate

My indoor refreshment table (Photograph: Alan Young).

properly and have a proper chat as we were in 'race mode'. This issue would get worse as the race progressed and we all became increasingly tired and frustrated with each other. There is no fault associated with this, we were all just concerned about *time*.

In long ultras, time can be frittered away very easily and quickly. One's whole sense and awareness of time changes during these events and not in a good way. Every task starts to take longer. Short chats become long chats. Moving around takes longer. Changing your socks on day one takes a couple of minutes, on day seven, it's 20 minutes.

It was after a few days that I noticed that the slope was having a significant effect on my pace uphill. Yes, it was nice to trot the downhill, but you can never make up what you have lost on the uphill. I always used a mix of running and walking in these extended races and on this occasion, I inserted an additional walk break on the uphill portion of the lap.

It was sometime during the eighth day, that I was at the furthermost part of the course from the main building, when I experienced a very sudden and incredibly intense need to urinate. It was all I could do to hold it, as I sprinted to the Portaloo, positioned

just outside the main building. Overwhelmingly relieved to have made it in time, I stood there – and nothing happened – I couldn't go. Eventually, I did pass a few drops but it was very painful.

This was the first indication that I was developing a problem during the race, although at the time it wasn't clear to me what was going on. All I knew was that my attention and focus was being split between my need to maintain my performance schedule and manage my multiple, urgent pee stops.

This scenario gradually got more and more frequent, and by 'Sod's Law' I usually seemed to be at the furthermost point from the Portaloo, necessitating another unwelcome sprint down to reach it in time. No one wants to be sprinting with hundreds of miles in their legs. I was also having to cope with significant pain and the accompanied mental stress of my situation. It was like peeing razor blades or shards of broken glass and to pass a few drops became an agonising process. The 'urge to pee' was incredibly powerful, but when I let go a few drops at best would pass. As I was running along, I was trying to work out what was wrong with me.

In any other situation I would, of course, have just popped along to the doctor to get a diagnosis. But here I was committed to the race.

The race organisers provided medical cover and I had comprehensive medical insurance to fall back on, but I decided not to seek professional assistance. In my head, I was continually assessing my situation, performing a balancing act, believing that I could manage things in a way that would allow me to successfully stay in the race and then be able to get home, to have treatment in a more familiar environment.

As an ultra-runner for so many years, I had become hardened to pain, discomfort and suffering, to achieve my goals. My thresholds were incredibly high – maybe too high. For example, I never used the word 'pain', only referring to 'discomfort'. At times, my pit-stop frequency was becoming

Athens - The temperatures rose in the later stages of the 1,000 mile race (Photograph: Alan Young).

My daily distances had steadily fallen from a first-day peak of 90 miles / 145 km to between 53 – 60 miles / 85-95 km a day, as I struggled with my condition.

All thoughts of world records had long been abandoned, but I was still chasing a number of national and international age-group records, at a variety of split times and distances. On day 12, I was also still hopeful that I could actually reach 1,000 Miles, inside the 16-day, race time limit.

The last straw was when I became urinary incontinent, during my sleep breaks. I didn't feel that I could share this with my crew. It just felt too

ridiculous, with me having to dash every other lap or so.

One day I saw a helper moving 'my' Portaloo on to a truck. "What are you doing with it?" I asked. "Taking it away; it's not needed anymore," was the response. I was gutted, as it had been so convenient for me. Now I would have to use the indoor loos, which weren't so hygienic and a little off the course too.

I was still perplexed about what I was suffering from. I asked the crew to Google my symptoms, but they didn't come back with anything for me. I discovered that sitting down to pee made it slightly less painful. I always travelled with a course of antibiotics, for urgent situations. I took them, but they had no effect, ruling out a urinary tract infection. My short naps were being interrupted and hence my recovery was insufficient, leaving me haggard and excessively tired, as I started each new run period.

My late night calls home to Jessica became increasingly fraught. She was also mentioning a growing alarm about an impending pandemic approaching Britain and asked me to take extra care with personal hygiene when I travelled home.

Battling intense bladder pain was the big issue during the 1,000 mile race (Photograph: Alan Young).

personal, a step too far. I grabbed old towels to wrap around myself, rinsing them when I awoke and draping them over anything I could find. I was completely unprepared for such a situation. I had no pads, insufficient underwear, no means of caring for myself. I suffered in silence. I felt wretched.

As the days went by, my symptoms worsened. By day 14, the levels of pain and discomfort I was having to handle were becoming overwhelming, both mentally and physically – even for me. This was the worst I had ever experienced. I just prayed for the race to be over and to get home, somehow. This couldn't continue.

It didn't have to. The race came to an end on the scheduled day 26. No extra time was allowed. I had to settle for 941.38 miles / 1,515.004 kms. I dreaded not being able to stay long enough at the awards ceremony without having to dash off, yet again, to the bathroom. Somehow, I managed it.

I planned to leave the race site very early the next morning, in order to arrive at the airport in very good time. I will be forever grateful to Erica Clarkson and her husband Adam for gifting me a taxi from the

I managed to hold it together until the race finished
(Photograph: Alan Young).

race to Athens airport – a 70-mile journey. It saved me waiting for a bus and then having to cope with a bumpy, long drawn out bus journey.

I was extremely anxious about the journey home and how I would be able to manage my toilet needs, while negotiating three airports and three flights home to Orkney. I had already stuffed my underwear with paper towels and there was little else I could do.

On the flight from Athens, I told the hostess that I had a bladder problem and would be making more frequent use of the toilet than is normal and also staying in there longer than usual. It was a case of no sooner had I returned to my seat, than I would be needing to go again. Meanwhile, toilet queues would build up, as it took me so long to pass a few drops.

Coming in to land in London, the hostess was urging me, through the toilet door, to return to my seat, but I couldn't do that as quickly as she would have liked.

More drama followed on the next leg of the journey as my plan to sit close to the plane toilets came adrift. On the flight from London to Edinburgh, I was pretty sure the toilets were at the front of the plane, so I asked for a seat as near the front as possible. Bugger! They were right at the back.

At least I was back in the UK, albeit still at the wrong end of it. I was struggling to cope with an unrecognised, but acutely painful bladder issue. I was cringing in pain and nursing my urinary incontinence and ever-distending abdomen. I was desperate to receive urgent medical care in my home town, among those I knew and trusted.

The 12-hour journey had been appalling and when I finally got back to Orkney I urgently presented to my GP. After one look at my lower body, she ordered me to A & E, her face aghast. Otherwise, a ruptured bladder was a possibility. Luckily, it was a short walk away, in the same building. I felt at once embarrassed, ashamed, drained and exhausted, confused and yet desperate to be relieved of my distress.

Following the treatment by Dr Gandiya, I was soon away home, feeling shocked and interfered with, a plastic tube emerging from the hole in my lower abdomen and a plastic bag strapped to my leg. I had been fitted with a supra-pubic catheter to enable me to pass urine, comfortably, direct from my bladder. That stayed in place for six long weeks, during which I couldn't run a step. When I tried, there was just too much bleeding into my bladder. However, I eventually made a full recovery after a subsequent prostate operation in February, 2021, a year later.

My race in Athens had ended in disaster, of course – albeit I was a mere 60 miles short of the 1,000-mile target – but I had some consolation inasmuch as I'd conquered 1,000 miles in Athens ten years before in the 2010 World Cup, when my multiday, ultra-running career was in its infancy.

Back then, I'd often sensed that the iconic 1,000-mile event could be one of my best, if only I could find the races to test myself. I felt that I had the required combination of relative speed and multiday, endurance experience to even, maybe, challenge the Scottish all-time record of the legendary, Canada-based, Al Howie, 12 days, 1 hour, 47 minutes. I was excelling at six-day races at this time and clocking up distances that even Howie never achieved.

But, those of us dedicated to these ultra-long races have a problem. We need people to organise them for us. It's often an unappreciated task. Runners can be fussy. They want a flat course, a good even surface, not too many twists and turns to hurt their exhausted bodies. They need a 24-hour food and drink supply and somewhere quiet and comfortable to rest and sleep. And, of course, that place mustn't be too far from the course. They don't want to waste time going to and fro, before and after their rest breaks. The number of competitors will be relatively small but entry fees must not be unpalatably high and good weather also helps, of course. And so the list of requirements goes on… and consequently, races are not plentiful.

The fact that both my attempts at 1,000 miles, were not only both in Athens, but ten years apart, indicates how hard it was to find suitable races.

My first attempt – with Howie's record firmly in my sights - was over a smooth, almost flat, 1 km, level, tarmac loop, on the site of the former Athens airport, which had subsequently been re-developed for the Olympics. The field was a small but accomplished group of eight, hardened athletes, five men and three women and, though I was the oldest, I was relishing my first attempt at this iconic distance. We had 16 days to achieve our goal, but some of us hoped to be finished long before that.

I'd spent weeks grappling with the mental challenge of suddenly running almost twice as far as I'd ever gone before. Not the way I usually liked to do things. Slow and steady was my approach, carefully increasing my endurance and experience over the previous sixteen years.

Sometimes, my gradual, painstaking approach wasn't possible and this was one such instance. My skill was in breaking races down into small, manageable chunks, which took the fear out of them, for me, anyway. I had to apply that logic to this one. I decided to focus entirely on my three or four-hour 'work periods', as I called them. The time blocks, when I would be on the course, running and walking. Run, then short, efficient break, then back on the course and run. Then repeat and repeat, *ad nauseam*.

I trained myself not to think ahead, if at all possible. If I found myself peeping forward in time, I would immediately drag my attention back to the present moment, knowing that distance was being accumulated, in an efficient and timely manner. A manner that can be repeated, day in day out. Week in, week out. A manner that will extend my endurance, allow me to recover, step by step and lead me to achieve unimaginable distances. This was my chosen mindset. This is how I would handle this huge jump in difficulty.

The overwhelming favourite was Germany's Wolfgang Schwerk. A supreme multiday specialist with a stellar CV going back as far as 1981. In addition, the experienced Italian, Lucio Bazzana, had impressive personal bests from 24-hour and 48-hour events and another German, Hans-Jürgen Schlotter, had a splendid six-day best distance, recorded just two years before.

On the whole, I generally ignore my main rivals. However, it is a race and if a crew member alerts me to a developing, competitive situation in the later stages, I will revert to 'race mode' and run to stay ahead of a closing rival. Essentially, I trained myself to just focus on my own race. I could do no more.

I passed 96.9 miles / 156 kms in the first 24 hours. That included a three-hour sleep and several 30 minute naps, between 'work periods'.

I was pleased with that and furthermore, I had established a good blueprint for the days ahead.

I had a small tent on the side of the road which I used for my naps, when it wasn't too hot. I then used the large sports hall for my longer sleeps, which were initially at night. Alan Young and Tim Rainey were getting into a good crewing rhythm, building in their own rest and sleep breaks, around mine.

Days passed and it was only on day four, that I slipped under 80 miles / 128 kms for the first time, recording 78.3 miles / 126 kms. I have always noticed that I can respond well in a competitive environment. If I have a distance or time target to chase, or a fellow competitor, for that matter, I can raise my game to meet that challenge. This happened in Athens. The first big challenge was

Athens 2010: Receiving refreshment from Tim Rainey and Alan Young.

It was tough in the heat of Athens 2010.

to try and reach 497 miles / 800 km in the first six days. That distance is the benchmark for world-class performance in standalone six-day races, let alone as a split distance in a 1,000-mile race.

By pushing myself to an 86.4 mile / 139 kms, sixth day, I was delighted to be able to slide over the 800km mark for only the third time in my career. Celebrations had to be short lived, as I still had a long way to go. One thousand miles is 1,609 kms. I was slightly less than half way to my target distance. However, my pace was strong.

Up until the day before the race started, it was cold in Athens. In fact, I had been down on the nearby beach wearing my Angora hat and gloves, so I can confirm that, they do indeed, have winter in Greece!

However, no sooner had the race started, than spring arrived with a vengeance. The sun was hot and strong and we had no shelter on the course. Feeling very much exposed, for such long hours on the road, was tough. My tent became far too hot to rest in. Initially, shade temperatures reached the mid-20s°C in the afternoons, but it felt much hotter in the unremitting sunshine. Night times became warm too, temperatures never falling below about 10°C.

Quickly, we noticed that as the weather warmed up, I was covering more distance at night, compared to the comparable time periods during the day. It then made sense to switch my long sleep, from the night to the day, thus enabling me to have more productive running hours in the cooler evening and night temperatures.

Day seven saw a drastic drop in distance for me, to only 51.6 miles / 83 kms. This was a heavy blow to my attempt on Al Howie's record and effectively put it beyond my reach.

Unwittingly, I had been tending to over-drinks and Dr Baxevanis put me on a diuretic medication that helped me to unload the excess fluid. This necessitated additional and longer rest breaks, which completely disrupted my clockwork-like rhythm and messed with my distance targets.

Athens 2010: Grinding out the miles.

Furthermore, I had rashly agreed to be part of a research project during the race. As a result, medical students started stopping me and others, briefly, to take blood pressure readings. Bizarrely, they were then surprised that our blood pressures were raised during running and we were instructed to rest, against our will, until the readings had reduced. I felt powerless and very disappointed, but decided I could do no more than comply. Eventually, they seemed to lose interest in the project and with great relief, I could run freely once again without hindrance.

My eight-day distance immediately jumped to 72.7 miles /117 kms, as my competitive juices were stirred and I pushed for a good 621 miles / 1,000 kms time.

A lot can happen in a 1,000-mile race, as I was about to find out. Even things that had never happened to me before. On a high, after passing 1,000 km the day before, I was optimistic about making further strong progress on day nine.

It wasn't to be.

My crewman, Alan Young, now operating alone as Tim had returned to Manchester for work, would often run in and out of the main concourse building. Then, one day in the early afternoon, as the heat of the day was building up, Alan failed to notice that the large plate-glass swing doors were closed and ran into them at full tilt. Thinking he was just stunned, he continued out of the building, down the steps and met me with a drink, as I completed another lap.

I was met by a 'Frankenstein-like' figure, with his head and face covered in blood, which ran down on to his clothing. Alan was completely unaware of his appearance.

He was led away to a medical facility as I raced on not knowing what had happened. This meant, of course, that I was left on my own and had to largely look after myself for some time. I could do this, but I lost momentum and focus and substantial distance as a result. Neighbouring support crews saw my predicament and came to my aid, when they could, especially the Finns, who were stationed nearby.

Alan re-appeared some hours later, with colourful tales of the Greek healthcare service, but my distance for that day plummeted, unsurprisingly, to 52.8 miles / 85 kms.

The grizzled Italian, Lucio Bazzana, was running a gutsy race and seemed to be getting stronger as the event progressed. However, that was unbeknownst to me, until Alan casually mentioned that Bazzana was running well and seemed to be closing on me. That was like a 'bolt from the blue' and I felt like I had been kicked up the behind.

I had been so much in the moment, that I hadn't given much thought to anyone challenging my current second place. To my horror, a short time later, Alan suddenly yelled "he's coming up behind you, now!" I simply couldn't believe that a competitive situation had suddenly developed, at this point, on day 11.

I felt a sudden spurt of adrenaline hit my brain and

The race suddenly became very competitive in 2010 when the experienced Italian Lucio Bazzana almost caught and overtook me late on in the race. I managed to break him and ended up finishing 11 hours ahead of him.

I was jolted into action. I jerked forward, increasing my pace and kept distance between myself and the chasing Bazzana. The normal routine of run, walks and drinks every lap was suddenly abandoned and I was now racing to keep not only ahead of Bazzana but to put some real distance between us, once again. With my head down and in deep focus, I managed to maintain my increased pace for long enough to seemingly break Bazzana and keep hold of my second place.

In fact, I did break him! He ended up finishing the race over 11 hours after me. He lost almost half a day to me over the closing 48 hours. These ultra-long races are a fascinating blend of mental and physical strength. As the event progresses, we have to marshal our resources as we go along.

Almost done! Approaching the finish line of the 1,000 Mile race in 2010. (Photograph: Alan Young).

Eking out every morsel of physical and mental energy, as we accumulate unimaginable distances, step by endless step.

Following the drama of day 11, day 12 dawned bright and hot. The end was in sight, but as always, it had to be focused on, lap by lap. This would inexorably bring that 1,000-mile distance. I ran well on this penultimate day, recording 64.6 miles / 104 kms, slightly more than day 11.

With the arrival of day 13, I knew that, barring a disaster, I would finish, it was just a case of when. In the intense mid-morning sunshine of Monday, March 29, I breasted the tape in 13 days 20 hours 8 minutes and 1 second.

In fact, I had been able to increase my average pace, once again and produced 73.3 miles / 118 kms in my final 24 hours. That's as near as one can

get to a sprint finish, in this type of event. I also set new World Age-Group records for 1,000 km and for 1,000 miles, along with many more records, at intermediate times and distances, at British and Scottish level, including age-group ones.

As expected, Schwerk won the race, just squeezing under 12 days, an outstanding performance.

My notes from the time, describing my recovery, give some indication of how my body reacted to its first 1,000-mile run.

"I aged by 30 years, over the first 7 days, post race. Appetite increased 100 per cent; sleep requirement increased 50 per cent. Sitting and lying were over-ridingly attractive.

Day 8 post-race: started making better progress.

Progressed well in week 2, post-race, ending with an hour-long beach walk on the second Sunday.

My lap of honour. 1,000 miles completed for the first time, in 13 days 20 hours 8 minutes and 1 second – a new World Age-Group record. (Photograph: Alan Young).

Afternoon sleep is naturally reducing to 30-60 minutes (from 2hrs) and appetite is reducing too. Body weight, 58.9kg, is almost back to my normal 60.2kg, on day 10, post-race.

Considerable thigh girth lost. Upper body very weak on return to training – could hardly do any pull-ups with body weight only."

Gathering world-class records

... 'it became an obsession' ...

I'm proud to say that at the time of writing, May, 2022, I still hold all the outright British, distance running road records, for greatest distance covered in 14 – 52 days and the fastest times to cover 2,000 kms right up to 5,000 kms.

During my competitive athletic journey, I became an unashamedly avid collector of running records but, perhaps strangely, it was only in the latter stages of my career that "record getting" became obsessive.

In my early days of ultra-running, I focused on the 100-km events and times that would gain me selection for Scottish and GB national teams. I made my debut in the British team, for the 1996 World 100-km Championships in Moscow.

When I moved up to 24-hour running, the race arrangements and my mindset were very similar. I made my debut, for the GB 24-hour team in Uden, Holland, in October, 2000. In my head, I knew what I was doing and why.

After I won my debut six-day race in 2006, I made the decision to focus on multiday running. I recognised that this would have serious consequences for me. It would mean losing financial support from UK Athletics, as races longer than 24 hours are not supported and funded by the national governing body, and consequently my National Lottery funding would vanish too.

Financially, I would be going it alone. The whole structure under which I operated for the previous ten years would fall away. There would be no firm targets each year of World and European Championships to aim for and of fully funded trips to those events. I began to realise that I had to find a new raison d'etre for my racing.

Sometime later my crewman, Alan Young, casually mentioned that I had made a number of ultra-running records. I hadn't realised this. I thought

nothing more of it at the time, but this revelation rattled around my mind for a while. Eventually, I cottoned on to the fact that breaking records could provide me with the new focus and ambition my race running required.

However, identifying records was one thing, finding suitable races in which to try and break them was another issue altogether. Sometimes, I would travel a long way, to New York for example, only to find that the event experienced appalling weather conditions with high winds and torrential rain for many days, scuppering any chance of a top record-breaking performance.

In the world of athletics, 'masters athletes' (those over the age of 35) are classified in five-year age bands, from the age of 35 and onward. As a result, masters athletes are possibly one of the very few groups of people who actually look forward to their next birthday, especially if it means they will then have a chance of success in their new higher age-group!

For me, every time I entered a new age-group it meant another raft of opportunities for records at all the different distances and times. As I progressed up through the age-groups the performances I had to beat became slower and shorter as competitors suffered the effects of ageing. Of course, Mother Nature had not given me immunity to this!

I made certain that races in which I chose to make record attempts had officially measured courses, authenticated by a national governing body. The task of rooting out these races worldwide was a time-consuming job and I'm indebted to Alan Young, Andy Milroy, Adrian Stott and 3,100-mile race director Sahishnu Szczesiul, who assisted me in finding records to chase and then documenting my performances when the records had been achieved.

In addition to hunting for suitable races, I also had to hunt for more sponsors after the loss of GB lottery funding. It was a chance referral from the Orkney office of an Aberdeen oil company, Xodus, that gave me a lucky break in this quest. They put me in touch with an Edinburgh sponsorship agency called Red Sky Management, who explained that simply saying that "I want to break records" was far too vague for potential sponsors. They said I needed to give my aims and ambition a name of some sort that had wide appeal and could be easily understood.

That piece of gold-nugget advice launched *Project 60 @ 60*, an ambitious attempt to set 60 ultra-distance running records, on road, track or indoors, at World, British or Scottish level, including age-group records, before I was 60.

Project 60 @ 60 was born on October 1, 2010, my 57th birthday. I had given myself three years to do it. The Press, the general public and sponsors identified with my 'project' enthusiastically. It was an easy handle for the 'man in the street' to grasp and enabled people to interpret and assess how well I was doing.

Personally, I thought it was a 'stretch goal' and it felt like I had put my neck on the line. But I needn't have worried. I achieved my goal in record time, no pun intended. At the Monaco eight-day race, in November, 2012, two 1,000km records enabled me to surpass the record target, 11 months ahead of schedule.

This emboldened me and in September, 2013, I announced a new target of 165 records before I was 65 in 2008 – *Project 165 @ 65*.

By now, I was researching my races very carefully, seeking out suitable, approved events that were worth attending. Record-chasing was really framing my season in a big way now.

Sometimes I would run well, but the weather conditions ruined any chance of records. On occasion, I would set no records for a year or more and then a hatful would come from one race. On other occasions, I missed potential records by mere minutes or metres because my exhausted support crew had omitted to alert me. It also hadn't escaped my notice that the longer the race, the more opportunities there were to set records.

This led me, inexorably, to the world's longest race in 2014, the Sri Chinmoy 3,100-miler in New York, where I clocked up another 54 records.

At last, in November, 2015, while competing in the Bislett Indoor International Endurance Festival, 48-hour race in Oslo, Norway, I set 21 new age-group records, including the World Over 60 record for completing 196.1 miles / 315.565 kms in 48 hours, indoors. This pushed me over the 165 records target, almost three years ahead of time.

As well as my age-group records, I was picking up many outright records for durations and distances in longer races.

Having achieved the 165 target, I didn't rush into setting any more targets for some time. I was unsure how I was going to proceed and what records I thought I could tackle, including my own. Eventually, two years later, in May, 2017, I settled on an audacious target of 750 records in a project I called simply *Journey to 750*, with no time limit.

Just days after I launched it publicly, my wife Elizabeth unexpectedly fell ill and it was almost three months after that when I felt able to return to competition with a 48-hour road race in the west of Hungary at the end of September, 2017.

Although my return to the Sri Chinmoy Self Transcendence 3,100-mile race in June, 2018, is generally considered as a 'failure' because I just ran out of time and 'only' managed 2,904 miles, in fact it was actually a record bonanza for me. During the first part of the race, when the temperatures were cooler, I had a flying start and for 27 days I was ahead of my injury-affected, first half, 2014 performance. The race director, Sahishnu Szczesiul, encouraged me to claim a host of single-age records and overall I set 200 new records in that race, giving my 'Journey to 750' hunt a huge boost.

In October of that year I graduated to the over-

Athens 2020. I've achieved my life-time target of setting over 750 records at World, British and Scottish level, including age group records. (Photograph : Alan Young).

65 age grouping. By becoming the first person to run the North Coast 500-mile route, I was able to claim a few more records, but it was when I completed the Milwaukee's six-day indoor race in August, 2019, that I was really able to boost my records tally. I came home with another 23 records, including the World Age-Group record for six-days indoor. This bumped up my total to 716, including 45 World Age-Group records.

When I travelled to Athens in January, 2020, for the 1,000-mile race, one of my main aims was to achieve my 750 record target and finish the race. I have devoted another chapter to this event but, in short, I achieved one of the two but I left Athens with a total of 773 records, including 104 World Age-Group records.

I had breached the magical number of 750!

Training and retrospection

… 'I focus more on recovery now' …

One of the most common questions I get asked, after "when are you going to retire?" is "how do you do it?" People glance at me, and see a small, slim man, appearing quite young for his age, but otherwise seemingly quite unexceptional. I exhibit nothing, outwardly, that might lead one to believe I have demonstrated quite extraordinary powers of endurance.

My approach to training was unique, and in this chapter I'll tell the story of how this produced the performances that have gained international attention. I'll explain how I developed my treadmill and cross-training, how I coped with injury and subsequently changed my running technique. How my developing home gym became a feature of my preparation and how reading one book sharpened my approach to race preparation in a very significant way and led to a 'purple patch' in my running career.

I had always been fascinated, by mental and physical training. How different trainers and coaches, in the same sport, could produce champions by seemingly different methods and approaches. How different countries often excelled in different sports, possibly due to cultural and ethnic differences, or simply determined by the way sports funding was allocated.

I wanted to apply the different training methods to myself to see what happened. I wanted to know how I could train myself to achieve my sporting ambitions and be the best that I could be.

I was a glutton for information, for research results, for knowing how others trained. When I was awarded National Lottery funding in 1997, I had to name a coach. David Murrie, Head of Sport and Exercise Science at Sunderland University, agreed to fulfil that role and we worked together for some years. Apart from David, I've been self-coached

Undergoing performance testing at the Sports Science Department of Sunderland University.

my whole running career, but well advised, at all times, from a variety of sources.

In the early days of my running career (Chapter One) I experimented with various training methods, including the use of weighted vests which worked very well. Sadly, I had to give them up as they seemed to aggravate a hip injury.

Over time, my settled training schedule was based on four running sessions a week. Typically, a continuous fast run on Saturday morning, a long steady run on Sunday morning, then much higher intensity sessions on Tuesday and Thursday. I would do non-running, cross-training on the other days. This was the basis of my training throughout my ultra- running career, although I introduced short periods of more race-specific training in 2009.

With experience, I came to value consistency of training, over specific, crushing workouts. To me it was better to train in a way that you could maintain, consistently, over a long period of time rather than spectacular sessions that increased the chance of being laid up for weeks.

Also, on balance, I favoured focusing on the process of training, over too much obsession with goals. Goals were important as signposts or as a compass in my sporting career, but of greater value was my attention to my day-to-day, week-to-week and month-to-month training. It's what I did on a regular and routine basis that determined what happened in my races.

Lottery Funding was a massive boost for me, as money had always been tight. This extra funding (£3,000) opened more doors for me as regards access to additional support services such as sports nutrition expertise. The most useful was to have two weeks warm weather training, initially in Majorca, in March each year.

National Lottery funding allowed me to experience 'Warm Weather Training' for the first time. Here I'm in Puerto Pollensa, Majorca in March, 1998.

Puerto Pollensa in northern Majorca was my location of choice in the late 1990s. It was an easy going town at that time of the year, with quiet country roads to run on, nearby access to some hills and a reasonable gym for treadmill sessions and cross-training. Elizabeth would accompany me on these trips, at our expense, and it provided a very welcome break after a long winter at home and set me up well for my upcoming race programme.

Unfortunately, on our third visit, it was cold in late March with snow on the hills! Our apartment

wasn't equipped for wintry weather with cold marble floors and no heating. The owner had to bring round portable heaters for us and additional blankets and we couldn't eat out on the veranda.

By good fortune, the mother-in-law of the UK's number one marathon runner at the time, Dan Robinson, had a holiday home in Sanday. On Dan's first visit to her in Orkney, I was able to meet up with him and mentioned my dilemma. He promptly suggested the small town of Playa Blanca in Lanzarote, in the Canary Islands. He had been there for exactly the same purpose and said it would be ideal.

I took his advice and Playa Blanca became my warm weather training location for a number of years. Down on the southern tip of the island, it was well suited to Elizabeth and I, with a good range of accommodation and services. The weather was very reliable but it was always windy, which of course we were used to. But there it was a really warm wind!.

Cross-Training. This refers to any training I did that wasn't running. I started doing this in 1994. In those days it was very unusual for a runner to be doing any form of cross-training, but I was very open minded about doing it.

I had been used to cross-training in my table tennis days and it made sense to toughen and strengthen the body and mind in ways that could support and enhance the running training.

I believe that my long history of cross-training has contributed to my many years of injury-free running and to my longevity in the sport

There were three key milestones in my career between 2001 and 2007: I got my first treadmill in early 2001; I sustained my first, significant running injury; and I changed my running technique.

My first treadmill was a cheap one, but the best I could afford at the time. I got it from the Empire Stores mail order catalogue and was able to pay for it in monthly installments.

This was a game-changer for me in so many ways.

Firstly, it freed me up from the limitations of the severe weather conditions sometimes experienced in Sanday, a very exposed island, with little shelter from the strong winds. Secondly, it enabled me to train when I wanted to, independent of daylight hours. In winter in Orkney, the days are short with dawn at around 8am and dusk about 3.30pm. As an early riser, having the treadmill opened up the first part of the day for me. I could get my training all done and dusted, by 9am on weekdays and Saturdays and 10am on a Sunday. Thirdly, the treadmill gave me full control of my training and helped me to maintain and develop my high-intensity sessions, as I could set the speed, the incline and the duration. I loved the training precision that the treadmill offered me and I've loved it ever since, as a versatile training tool.

I was often asked "How do you train for such long races, on your tiny island?" Well, the answer lies in the fact that most of my key training sessions were done on the treadmill, with just longer, easier runs done on the road on a Sunday morning.

My poor treadmill got battered to bits with my regular training and I was grateful to the local handymen who came along and fixed it the best they could. In the end, the whole headboard had been reconfigured and wires were hanging out all over the place, as the various switches had been replaced to keep it going. Later on, around 2007, I was able to upgrade a bit.

The manager of the Pickaquoy Leisure Centre in Kirkwall was showing me the new, state-of-the-art, treadmills that were being installed in the centre's gym. In all innocence, I asked "what's happening to the old ones?" "That will be a council matter," he replied. As the old treadmills were top-quality, heavy-duty professional models, but without the fancy screens and media connections current users wanted, I was immediately interested in trying to get hold of one if I possibly could.

To cut a long story short and to their credit, Orkney Islands Council gifted me one of the treadmills. It was a huge thing for me and lasted until I left Sanday in 2019, when I gifted it to another ultra-

runner in Orkney, as I had nowhere to house it at the time.

My home gym in Sanday developed gradually over the years and was eventually moved up to the far end of my business unit, an area that only had skylights, but that didn't bother me. As well as my treadmill, it housed an exercise bike, a set of weights and various mats, exercise balls, and foam rollers.

Some years later, I had it lined with silver foil and created my own climate chamber with a large patio heater in front of the treadmill, fans, a dehumidifier and room humidifiers to train for races in hot and humid conditions.

Sanday has a small population of around 500 people and every time new folk came in, they would bring new skills and experiences with them. Shaun Brassfield-Thorpe brought techniques in the ancient, Norwegian marshal art called 'Stav', an interest in Norse mythology, massage skills and fitness training experience, as a former gym manager in Berkhampsted in Hertfordshire.

Training with Shaun in my animal shed gym.

I made contact, initially for the purpose of getting a sports massage, but he soon became a twice-weekly visitor to my gym, where he would supervise my weight training. Over the next eight years, Shaun played a significant role in guiding my strength development. This was largely by means of using increasingly heavy loads and doing 'partials', which is where the bar is moved just a few millimetres off the stands for a few seconds. By doing this I was able to bear a crazy amount of weight, for fractions of a second, with Shaun supervising ("spotting") me.

Spotting is where another bigger, more experienced person, stands behind the lifter, ready to assist if they're not able to handle the load safely. As Shaun was twice as big as me in height and girth, he was the ideal spotter. I would be strapped up from head to toe, in hip, knee and ankle supports, to help keep me rigid and safe during the lifts.

In the early years of my running career I'd had all the usual aches and pains you might expect, but nothing that really affected me for more than a few days. However, after winning a 12-hour track race in Sheffield, in August, 2001, I was 'cock a hoop' and as soon as I came home, I did a hard training run wearing my weight vest. That was a bad mistake and I sustained a right shin injury. I had allowed insufficient recovery time and I had paid the price.

The tendon injury proved hard to recover from. I followed the lengthy protocols laid down by the Physio Department at the local hospital in Kirkwall. I used my treadmill to carefully build up my running and walking, but every time I returned to continuous running, the shin tendon flared up again.

Months went by and I felt like I was getting nowhere. Eventually, the physio said it was time to try a cortisone injection into the tendon sheath. This was performed by my local GP and it worked like a miracle! I returned to a mixture of running and walking and eventually to steady, pain-free running. The injury never recurred, but I had lost almost a year of racing.

It was a hard lesson to learn and it never happened again.

During my year out of racing I successfully changed my running technique. My aim was to develop a more efficient running style. I watched DVDs of the Greek, ultra-running great, Yiannis Kouros, to see how he ran. I tried to learn from him and developed a more efficient shuffling style with minimal knee lift which I could maintain consistently for days at a time in an ultra race.

In 2009, I started to organise my own "Training Camps", as I called them, to make the training for my races more specific. A kind of dress rehearsal and a bit like boxers' "Fight Camps" before a big fight.

I would typically get the ferry to Kirkwall, check into a hostel and then run and walk for multiple hours a day, on a lap course in a nearby park. I'd do this for at least two or three days in order to get realistic feedback from the experience. This feedback could then be applied in my races.

Initially, this was to test my troublesome race nutrition planning, but I soon realised that it had great physical and mental benefits too. I was able to test different ratios of rest and running and of running and walking. I was able to hone my mental focus and concentration, while lapping the park for long hours in strong winds. As well as being able to focus in and find my weaknesses, I was also able to identify my strengths; I discovered that once my pace slowed to a certain speed, thereafter, I didn't slow down much more. I was able to hold that speed for countless hours, somehow.

I also found that these intense training periods mimicked race demands more constructively than just grinding out high weekly mileages. I was a relatively frequent racer, but if I hadn't raced for two or three months, then I would slot in a training camp to fill the gap. The camps became a key part of my training strategy, as did the races themselves.

This unusual form of training didn't go unnoticed around Kirkwall. On one occasion both Shaun and Alan Young were supporting me when we had a visit from the local constabulary, in the small hours, as they had received a report of 'suspicious activity' in the park!

For my training to be effective, it had to be balanced with appropriate recovery. My approach to recovery changed gradually over the years, but often it took the form of simply not doing the training that I would normally do and just having days off.

When I became a committed ultra-runner, I installed a three-week running break, at some point every year, usually at the end of the season. I would do beach walks and cross training during those weeks, but no running. I always sensed that this was beneficial.

I remember first becoming aware that some other runners didn't have my recovery mindset when at a 24-hour race in Phoenix, Arizona in 2004, my first event in the USA. I had won the race, covering 136.39 miles / 219.50km and I was looking forward to a week's rest while being a tourist and visiting the Grand Canyon for the first time.

My crew and I were just loading our bags into our hire car, the morning after the race, when I was surprised to see a runner shuffling slowly past us. I recognised him as having been in the race with me. I wandered over to another runner, loading his vehicle as we were, and asked him, what the guy was doing. "Oh, he's a 'streak' runner" he said. Feeling a bit naive, I asked what that meant. It meant he just ran every day and never took a break, for as long as possible. It could carry on for many months or years. I was told there are teams of runners who support each other doing this via internet groups and so on.

It was certainly a surprising revelation to me, at the time, but nowadays it is nothing unusual at all. While it isn't something I would want to do, I imagine it must satisfy a strong sense of routine and habit that some find attractive or even addictive.

I am fortunate to have had a 26-year career at the top level in ultra-running with minimal time-outs for illness and injury. The number-one factor that has

enabled my successful ageing as an athlete is my mindset.

I have known athletes who have simply been unable to accept they grow older and age. They throw their arms into the air and moan and complain about their times and distances being so bad now. They lament how much slower they are and speak about how fast they used to be. Many have egos that simply can't accept the changes that are coming about and they usually stop running and sink back into a frustrated retirement.

Of course, I glance back at my times and performances from yesteryear. I enjoy that thrill from far-off memories, but allow myself to move on and be comfortable with who I am now. In reality, there is no choice.

I have used this mindset successfully in my own ultra-running career, especially in my attitude to 'shorter' events. As I moved up in distance and became competitive at the mega, multiday ultra-marathons, I found that I lost my competitiveness in the 'shorter' races. For those events, I would focus on age-group rankings and records and this kept me motivated, enthused and active in the sport.

As I've grown older, I have found a greater need to focus on recovery and all that entails. I was approaching my early to mid-60s when I first sensed that one day's recovery between intense treadmill workouts was becoming an issue. I realised that recovery needed more time and changed my routine to allow more days between concentrated training sessions. Interestingly, despite needing a little more recovery time, I haven't needed to reduce the intensity itself.

When I was younger, it was easy to give scant regard to any talk of recovery. I thought of it as wasted training time and gave little thought to active recovery methods. To some degree, I got away with this type of thinking, when younger, but certainly not in later life. The different methods I have used to improve my recovery are described below. Except for focusing on sleep and naps, which I have always done, the others have depended on my living circumstances at the time and the facilities which have been available to me.

Sleep. This has been and always will be my most important recovery method. At different times in my life I've played around with reducing sleep to maybe 'save time,' but it never works, in the long term.

Naps. I would say that this has been the second most important way to enhance my recovery. I regarded it as a skill that I had to learn and I've used naps for more years than I care to remember. In long events, the ability to take regular short naps for sleep and digestion were part of my successful race planning.

Massage. For as long as I have been able to afford it, I have included a monthly sports massage as part of my recovery plans. I'm now able to increase it to twice monthly, which as far as I'm concerned is a good thing. A good masseur will work my muscles and surrounding tissues in a way not normally experienced. Often, they will find minor damage, tension or soreness that I didn't know existed and then treat it accordingly.

Epsom Salts baths. Since moving to a town house with a bath in 2020, this recovery method has become available to me. For me, it's the hot soaking for 20 minutes that seems to do the trick.

Sauna, Steam Room and Jacuzzi. Personally, I like heat in all its forms! For some years, I had a small, infra-red, sauna cubicle at my home, which I used regularly, especially if I was heading to a race in a hot climate. I now live near the Pickaquoy sports centre and utilise the health suite facilities there, a sauna, steam room and jacuzzi, which I use at least twice a week.

0-0-0-0-0

One key change that happened during my running career was the acquisition of my own travelling support crew. Up to 2004, I had always had to rely on volunteers provided by the race organisers. As I was quite well known in the sport, race directors were usually willing to get a local student or club member to support me for at least part of a race.

While this was very much appreciated, it was often far from ideal, largely because we didn't know each other and they might only appear now and then to help out.

On many occasions, I watched very enviously the superb crewing my opponents benefited from, often from their own family members. I recall that the French wives provided superb crew support for their husbands.

At one of my few trail races through the Scottish Highlands, Alan Young crewed for me, along with my daughter, Bella. Following the race, Alan offered to help me in any way I might suggest and on my long bus journey home from Fort William, it dawned on me that maybe he might consider crewing for me on a regular basis. He had explained that he was single, very early retired and had a healthy pension from Scottish Water.

Within a few days, Alan had been recruited as my personal support crew and he was willing to pay his own way as well. It turned out that we were the same age and were able to get on well, both on and off the course. He was very inexperienced at crewing and we both had much to learn over the coming 16 years at races around the world.

Crewing can be an unenviable job. Crew members are stuck at the side of the course in all weathers, often for days on end, trying to keep their runner moving at all times. They keep track of progress, monitor possible record possibilities, update media, prepare food and drink as directed and cope with the unexpected as well.

Alan told me how he often felt "powerless" when witnessing my often sudden and debilitating episodes of vomiting. I'm grateful for the many years of help and support he provided for me.

Over the years, I built up a trusted team of support personnel, including a physio, chiropractor, podiatrist and a masseur, to both treat issues when they occurred and to help keep me in tip top condition the rest of the time. I called them my "Team Sichel" and thought of them as a very worthwhile investment in myself.

I am obviously very appreciative of my support team, but I must also acknowledge the help of someone I have never met, Clive Woodward, who masterminded England's rugby World Cup triumph in 2003.

I stumbled across his book *Winning* and was struck by the minute detail that went into Woodward's planning before the actual tournament.

Putting some detail on the lengths they went to, in order to be ready, Woodward explained that they went to Australia a year before the planned matches and on the exact same days and time, they drove and timed the coach journeys from the team hotel to the match stadiums. By doing this, they could experience the possible traffic delays and plan accordingly. No stone was left unturned.

The book opened my eyes to the importance of detailed preparation and I realised that I was in a position to execute some of the ideas I had read about. Some key changes I made were in allowing more travel time to races. Acknowledging that travelling is tiring and delays can increase my stress levels, I began sleeping an extra night near Heathrow, instead of immediately jumping on to an overnight flight to save money. I also started arriving at the race destination two or three days prior to the competition. This allowed me to settle in and feel comfortable with the weather and local environment, before the gun went.

No book about my ultra-marathon racing career would be complete without mention of how I paced myself. It's as much an art, as a science.

When I first saw the later stages of a 24-hour race I asked "why are they all running so slowly?" "Because they've been running for 22 hours!" was the reply. It was only when I started running the longer ultras myself, such as the 24-hour and beyond, that I came to understand what it felt like.

It took me a long time to accept that I had to do some walking in races. Walking was anathema to me and I was, and still am, a slow walker. I had to watch and learn from others, more experienced than myself.

Winning the British 100 km Championships in July 1999 in Edinburgh.

I spent a period of months attempting to walk faster, but I didn't take to it very well at all. I discovered that at quite a slow speed, I was more comfortable running than walking. I was able to run slowly, but very efficiently and do a mix of running and walking, in order to extend my endurance and still be moving well in the final stages of events.

Understanding how fast to run in order to best cover the distance, or run the greatest distance in the allotted time, is the issue and it takes years of experience. Combining running and walking is the most common practice, but deciding how much to do of each can be a very long conversation.

I gradually increased my racing distances, from the 100km to the World's Longest Race, over a period of 20 years. I learned how to pace myself at each new distance. It was like climbing a staircase, spending a few years on each step and then going to the next one.

Pushing the pace during a 6-hour race in Sheffield in 2001.

Looking back … every athlete will reflect on his or her career and spot the highlights, as I have done in this book by dedicating chapters to certain races. But, of course, there are many other memories and "lesser" highlights that represented key, critical moments in my career and there are the inevitable low points and failures ….

From 2001 - 2002 I had been out of racing due to my shin injury – always a worrying time for any athlete – and I was keen to start competing again, hoping that I would return to the same performance standard I had already reached. I need not have worried, as I achieved third at my first outing in October, 2002, at the Road Runner's Club 100-mile track race at Crystal Palace in London.

Just a month later, I was then delighted to be able to do an event in my home county, Orkney. Running in the islands' Pickaquoy Leisure Centre, I set two Guinness World Records for treadmill

running. The first, for the fastest time to cover 100 miles and the second for the greatest distance covered in 24 hours.

Although the 24-hour event was my main focus then, I still mixed in other events as well and it wasn't long before my curiosity was piqued again and I was tempted to try a 48-hour race, with the usual "I'll give it a go" philosophy. My first 48-hour race was in Cologne, Germany, in July, 2003. This time it wasn't a winning debut and I only covered 158.30 miles / 254 kms, due to stomach problems.

I had hoped that by competing in 48-hour races, it might make my 24-hour results more consistent, but this didn't happen, largely due to continuing stomach issues. I notched up a variety of races in this time period, including my first run on the West Highland Way, the 'Devil of the Highlands' 43-miler, where I was runner-up to a Nepalese competitor.

Ice cream always went down well! This lot fuelled me to another 6-day victory in Hungary. (Picture: Alan Young).

Showing grit and determination running for my country in the Commonwealth 24-hour Championships in Keswick in September, 2009 while being cheered on by a young supporter. Thank you, whoever you are!

Every athlete has a "purple patch" or a "golden age" and 2006 – 2014 was mine in super long-distance running, with multiple victories and many personal best distances and records being recorded. I won a 24-hour race in Hull, a 48-hour race in Germany, a 72-hour race in Arizona, and a seven-day race in Greece and an eight-day race in Monaco.

Negotiating a muddy bend on a 400m cinders track following heavy rain at the 2008 Hamm 6-day race. I went on to win with over 532 miles. (Picture: Alan Young).

My six-day personal best peaked at 532 miles / 857 kms in Hamm, Germany, in the summer of 2008, with another six-day victory in Hungary. I found my niche in multiday running.

Those years were the golden ones but subsequent ones were far from uneventful.

In the home stretch of the 2009 Spartathlon race in Greece. Non-stop for 153 miles to take ninth place.

My crew support of Marja Hardus and Alan Young, shelter in the summer downpours at the Hamm 6-day track race in Germany.

I was honoured in 2012 to be asked to carry the Olympic torch on the final leg of its journey in Orkney, which ended with me lighting the cauldron at the Pickaquoy Centre in Kirkwall.

24 HOUR TRACK RACE

1	Jim Rogers 64	21	Steve Coote 36
2	Chris Finill 40	22	Ian McCuaig 55
3	Colin Jones 49	23	Bob Boies 31
4	Stefan Lindvall 54	24	Malcolm Knight 52
5	Chris Carver 33	25	Lorna Maclean 57
6	Richard Cunningham 37	26	John Maclean 36
7	William Sichel 67	27	Stef Lisowski 66
8	Sharon Gayter 43	28	Purna Seneuryn 62
9	Ken Fancett 39	29	Jorgen Schmoker 65
10	Matt Mahoney 58	30	Kathy Tytler 72
11	Eoin Keith 51	31	Katherine Kay-Austin 46
12	Bjoern Hrjonsturp 47	32	Gilbert John 48
13	Vicky Skelton 60	33	Richard Spyker 69
14	Geoffrey Oliver 61	34	Ray McCurdy 41
15	Adjarbaneil Adiba 30	35	Dave Green 45
16	Karl Fursey 42	36	Pamela Storey 79
17	Jeremy Mower 60	37	Dave Holloway 44
18	Sandra Brown 32	38	Patricia Comaniciu 59
19	Glen Keegan 50	39	Sue Clements 34
20	Rab Lee 53	40	Dan Coffey 35
		41	
		42	

Working my way up the score board in the Tooting 24-hour track race.

The 2014 – 2020 period included a wide variety of races, many chosen to assist me in my record setting ambitions. Races ranged from 24-hour events in London, Switzerland and Kirkwall, 48-hours indoors in Oslo, six-day events in Hungary and France, the iconic and world's largest ultra-marathon, the Comrades, in South Africa and a very high altitude race, La Ultra, in Ladakh, Indian Kashmir.

In 2018, I returned to New York for a delayed, second attempt at the 3,100. The summer of 2018 was oppressively hot, with multiple days reaching temperatures exceeding 35°C. I was okay up to 35 but, once the mercury exceeded that point, I was in trouble. Frequent trips back to my air-conditioned apartment to cool down were necessary, resulting in too much time lost. That time and distance couldn't be clawed back in the cooler evening hours, when I came into my own, running strongly to midnight every day. When the 52 day time limit was reached, I had recorded 2,904 miles. Despite everything, just 196 short of my goal.

My last ultra-marathon was the Athens Ultramarathon Festival 1,000-mile race in early 2020, detailed in chapter 11. I didn't know it would be my last one at the time.

The ultimate test

... 'I howled and cried' ...

My bag was by the door ....

It was 9pm on Monday evening June 12, 2017.

My 20kg bag was by the door. Months of planning was coming to a climax. Early the next morning I was embarking on a 3,000-mile, trans-Atlantic trip to the "Big Apple" - New York city. My second attempt at the world's longest race, the Sri Chinmoy Self Transcendence 3,100-miler awaited me.

I was in peak form. I was ready. Honed to perfection by previous experiences and months of specific preparation. Heat training in Sanday and a warm weather training spell in Santorini in Greece, an island my wife Elizabeth had always wanted to re-visit having had a day there on a Mediterranean cruise. My support crew of Alan Young and Tim Rainey were on their blocks and ready to go.

I felt the race field was slightly weaker than usual.

This was my chance. Twenty-three years of ultra-marathon training and racing were coming to a head and a podium finish in this epic race was within my grasp. It would be the crowning glory of my running career.

The phone rang on time, exactly when promised…

0-0-0-0-0

For many years previously, Elizabeth always described herself as a 'creaking gate'. Ever since a hospital stay for a perforated eardrum as a child, her medical issues had been ever-present. A bad back had terminated her promising nursing career. Serious sinus issues had dogged her throughout her adult life. Entering her late 40s and early 50s, arthritic conditions started to become an issue and interfered with her love of long vigorous walks. Multiple surgeries ensued, with first her left hip

In 2016, with Elizabeth's arthritis worsening, I wondered if there was anything she would really like to do while she could still travel? She responded "I'd love to see the wild animals in Africa!" Her dream was realised in January, 2017, when we were able to visit the Nairobi National Park in Kenya. She struggled with her health in Kenya and we thought it was the heat and the altitude. We now know that it wasn't just those environmental factors. I've always loved this photograph of her – displaying her love of colour and her attitude.

being replaced and then the right. Both knees followed and a shoulder operation too.

She was becoming well known at the Woodend Hospital in Aberdeen and on first name terms with some of the consultants. Soon her surgeries numbered 25 and still counting. She had become allergic to morphine, which caused alarming issues with post-operative pain control.

In the spring of 2017, Elizabeth remained under the weather for some weeks. Just coughs, colds and the usual sinus issues dragged her down and seemed endless. I was concerned and twice I offered to postpone my New York trip and do it another year. But Elizabeth was adamant, I was going to New York come what may. She said there was no question of me not going. We had a home help in place, in case that was needed. I agreed my plans would proceed.

We had a tradition that before really long races we would go on a mini-break, somewhere in Orkney, just for a few days as a couple. That year we spent some time in Orkney's South Isles, which were new for us being North Isles folk.

Walking around St Margaret's Hope, where streets are on different levels, requiring steps to be climbed, Elizabeth suddenly experienced breathlessness with frequent stops and starts as

Elizabeth pictured resting in St Margaret's Hope after feeling breathless while walking around the village in May, 2017.

we explored the village. I was concerned. This was a new, unexpected twist.

We got the bus back to Kirkwall and the same thing happened again, on the level walk from the bus station to the ferry. She said it was just her low blood pressure, but I said she had to see the island's GP the next morning. She did – but forgot to mention the breathlessness, having only spoken about her sinuses. A repeat visit the next day resulted in us both travelling back to Kirkwall for a hospital visit, immediately. The doctor wanted further investigations, as there was "a small shadow on the lung – probably an infection". An MRI was booked for early Monday morning and Elizabeth had to stay in hospital, much to her chagrin, while I returned to Sanday to finalise my preparations for New York.

She duly returned home off the Monday evening ferry and just said "the doctor will phone at 9pm to explain my results." She said nothing more and although concerned, I detected nothing in Elizabeth's demeanor that caused me alarm.

Elizabeth answered the expected phone call. The young doctor apologised profusely for having to break such news over the phone. Elizabeth put her at ease. "The MRI scan detected advanced lung cancer with a life expectancy of three to six months!"

I felt a lightning bolt surge through my body. I thought my head was going to explode. In a flash, New York was history and irrelevant. My time and place would be here with Elizabeth.

It was as if my whole sporting journey had prepared me for this moment. For all those years, my skills were developed to cope with the grinding routine of endurance training and competition but also the mindset to deal with disappointment, stress, crunch moments in sport. Now I was facing the ultimate test – an end-of-life scenario for my nearest and dearest. We take life so much for granted. Everyone we know is alive – until they aren't.

Never before had I experienced such a complete mindset change, in just a microsecond. The skills of being completely in the moment. Of breaking everything down into tiny steps. Of focusing on my breathing. My ability to relax under mounting stress and exhaustion. My stickability and bloody-mindedness had never been more needed now.

Even with this news, Elizabeth implored me to still go on my trip. She would get someone else to accompany her to the specialist centre in the Aberdeen Royal Infirmary. I simply dismissed such nonsense.

Upon diagnosis, Elizabeth very philosophically said that she had experienced a great life and had done everything she wanted and she wasn't going to 'fight' her condition. Furthermore, at a bedside discussion with our GP, myself, the local nurse and one of our daughters, Bella, she announced that she would like to attend the Swiss Dignitas assisted dying centre, in order to be able to die as soon as possible with dignity and without pain.

Our GP expertly relieved her anxiety regarding those matters and she agreed to travel to Aberdeen Royal Infirmary, as had been planned, as soon as they were ready to receive her, which was about a week later.

I was at her bedside multiple hours a day and noted down everything that was said in the daily doctor's rounds and what medications were administered by the nursing staff. It gave me something to do and was of great value to Elizabeth too. Initially,

I was with Elizabeth throughout her short final illness. We're pictured here at the Aberdeen Royal Infirmary.

we thought that following further scans, tests and palliative treatment we would be returning to Sanday, where she decided she wanted to die.

This wasn't to be. I gradually realised that we wouldn't be going anywhere fast. I noticed that the doses of all the pain medications were increasing daily. First there was a syringe pump in her left thigh, gradually administering medication. Then, a few days later, there was an additional one in her right thigh. I wasn't daft. I could see where this was going. A prognosis of three to six months now looked vastly optimistic.

By the end, she just managed the medical flight back to Kirkwall's Macmillan Ward in the Balfour Hospital, where she passed away peacefully a few days later.

She had died 24 days after diagnosis.

At the time, I thought it had been a long time from diagnosis to death. Later, I came to realise it hadn't been – it felt very, very sudden. There had been no time for me to come to terms with it and get used to the new reality. That had to come, gradually, in the ensuing months.

Returning to Sanday, I immediately did a 20-mile run, out and back, from Upper Breckan to the island's ro-ro pier. I hadn't run for a month – unheard of in my 25-year running career. I howled and cried into the wind, yelled out my grief and shock as I laboured up and down that lonely, hilly road.

This seemed to relieve the pressure trapped in my chest and lower body. The sheer physical exertion doing its work. My cheeks wet and my body exhausted, I returned to a now different Upper Breckan.

My run training gave me a vital structure and framework to re-build my life in Sanday. This proved highly beneficial and was an important tool in my journey to rediscovering myself as a single man.

Sometime later, poring over her medical notes, I was shocked to discover that she had been told

Over a period of years I've raised large sums for the Orkney
Cancer Charity, CLAN.

the news before returning to Sanday that Monday evening. Such was her desire not to disrupt my trip to New York, she had never told me, even though she knew the evening phone call would reveal all.

Eighteen months later I left my island home of the past 38 years and started a new life in the Orkney capital, Kirkwall.

Why?

Why did I do it? It's a very fair question considering the turmoils I went through, especially in my fairly early years of ultra-running.

I don't really think of myself as a very competitive person but I was one of nine children, so I must have stood my ground from time to time, although my older brother always had the better of me. My parents and siblings were mildly supportive but they were otherwise pretty much indifferent to my sporting endeavours. There was absolutely no pressure from home to achieve any kind of sporting success. Any competitive spirit I had was with myself, rather than with an opponent.

Looking back, there's no doubt in my mind now, that I unconsciously used 'trying hard at sports' as an ice-breaker, every time I had to go to another school – I attended six in total. I was small, late maturing and very shy and this proved to be a very effective way of gaining acceptance. I also enjoyed expending energy and 'doing my best'.

My motivation in running and ultra-running in particular, was underpinned by a passionate, personal curiosity which the sport lent itself to, with longer and yet longer events to try. These long events were an opportunity to delve deeply into my abilities and discover what I was best at.

A family Christmas in 2005. From left to right: my son-in-law Mike and daughter Tanya with Logan, Elizabeth, me and our other daughter, Bella.

Over time, I became fascinated by the demands of the different events in terms of how to keep going, how to manage fatigue and discomfort (my codeword for 'pain') both mentally and physically. At times, I was handling excruciating pain and fatigue. I clearly had a very high pain tolerance, but I found it got to a certain point I could take and then it got no worse. In effect, I was performing a balancing act with my assessment of my extreme discomfort. I made sure I never reached the point of total exhaustion.

I also derived a deep sense of satisfaction knowing that I was good at these super-long events and successful at doing them. In a strange way, I found them exceedingly enjoyable, despite the hardships involved. I never felt that I was doing myself any lasting harm in any way. I always monitored my recovery and was always reassured with how I coped and recovered.

My involvement in the sport also satisfied my enjoyment of travel and adventure. My running events took me to 22 countries and with the addition of my hitchhiking adventures in the early 70s, I have experienced 39 countries in all. I was very comfortable in foreign environments, foreign languages and foreign cultures.

Aged 69, I am still training hard and living in Kirkwall but race no further than the marathon (26.2 miles / 42.2kms) these days.

For full details of all my races and records
please contact my website at
www.williamsichel.co.uk